THE VEGAN SOULFOOD GUIDE TO THE GALAXY

- AFYA IBOMU -

Certified Holistic Health Counselor, AADP

Forward by Queen Afua

Author of *Heal Thyself* and City of Wellness

Photography By Afya

The Vegan Soulfood Guide to the galaxy

Copyright © 2008, by Afya Ibomu

ISBN-13: 978-0-9770092-2-0
ISBN-10: 0-9770092-2-X
Library of Congress Control Number: 2008930901
First edition 2008, Second edition 2010

Printed in Canada

Photography: Afya Ibomu
Cover and about the author photography: Khnum "stic.man" Ibomu
Interior and Cover Design/Layout: Shannon Washington
Illustrations: goldi gold
Editing: Details Count, Sis Abena Muhammed

Note to the reader: This book is to be considered as a reference work only, not a medical text. This material draws from the ancients systems as well as the author's own experience. The information contained in the following pages is in no way to be considered as a substitute for consultation, diagnosis or treatment by a duly licensed physician or other health care professional. This information is intended solely for use as a source of general information and not for application to any individual case. It is sold with the understanding that the publisher is not engaged in rendering medical advice. If you have a medical problem we urge you to seek a competent Holistic, Naturopathic or Medical health practitioner.

Published by:

Nattral Unlimited, LLC

PO Box 310330   Atlanta, Ga 31131

www.NATTRAL.com

nattral
health culture style
www.nattral.com

Get Your Crochet On! Hip Hats and Cool Caps

Get Your Crochet On! Fly Tops and Funky Flavas

Nattral Seasonal Detox: Spring

To
Alison
Be Healthy

Afya

This book has been a long time coming but it's finally here! I really want to give thanks to my family for their patience and understanding as the book was being finished. I'd also like to thank them for their input and willingness to be taste testers. I love you!

To my husband Khnum, thanks so much for your consulting, eye, input and experience in the book game. I love you!

To my mom, thanks for always being supportive and willing to help out in any way. Luv ya!

To my home girl Shannon Washington, this is book number 3!! You always know how to bring my vision to life with out me even having to say it! You are multitalented, creative and professional. Love ya homie! (shannonwashington.com)

I have such gratitude and appreciation for all of the healers I've worked with, learned from and came before me. Your wisdom and dedication to the health of our people is inspiring and necessary!

INTRODUCTION

I was inspired to write this guide in order to answer all of the questions I have received during the last eighteen years of being a vegetarian. Common questions have come up over and over again such as, "If you don't eat meat, what do you eat?" or "Where do you get your protein?" or "Isn't it expensive to eat healthy?" These questions, coupled with the health crisis in the black and brown communities, helped me realize that there is a need for more ways to educate our selves about incorporating healthier food choices into our lives. Too many people in our communities are dying unnecessarily and living poor qualities of life just because of the foods they eat. No doubt, we are oppressed; this daily reality causes our communities to have higher incidences of disease. Poverty, police brutality, racism (housing, jobs, education, health care, grocery stores), jail, drugs, single parent homes and the multitude of other issues that plague our communities, are negatively affecting our mental, physical and spiritual health—our holistic health.

One thing we can do to make a change in our lives is to begin with the food choices we make—because you are what you eat. Everything we put in our mouth becomes who we are, whether it's an apple, a Snicker's bar, a green juice or a Mickey-D's hamburger. These things become you. This very important fact is overlooked in our society and masked by corporate giants selling us Red Dye #40 and artificial strawberry flavor as a substitute for real strawberries that grow from the ground. In general, a vast majority of people in this nation do not get enough fruits and vegetables in their daily lives and consume an excess of processed foods (white flour, white rice, white sugar). This is where becoming vegetarian helps to improve your health. Studies show that eating fruits, vegetables, beans, nuts and whole grains, decreases your chance of getting heart disease, cancer, diabetes and a host of other ailments. Life can be wonderful, exciting, and even somewhat bearable if you feel well. But, if your head, heart, stomach and body are constantly hurting, your life changes and can seem somewhat overwhelming.

This guide has come through me as a result of my experiences with the medical industry, holistic health counseling, political education, vegetarianism, hip-hop and self-healing. Being vegan has helped to cure me of asthma, a so-called "incurable" disease, and many other ailments. It has expanded my knowledge of my own culture as well as other cultures through their food. It has also sharpened my political awareness of the food and drug industry. Governmental policies tracing all the way back to the White House, trickle down to affect our nutritional education, the food we see on the grocery shelves and ultimately, our personal food choices. One thing that I have seen and am sure of is that something is not working. People are not healing. The levels of obesity, cancer, diabetes, heart disease, osteoporosis and so many other daily discomforts that we deal with are enormous and do not seem to be declining. Most people are just sick, on drugs, eating whatever they want and living uncomfortably as long as their body can withstand the disease, drugs and lack of nutrients. Unfortunately, many times that fight is defeated too soon and we are losing our loved ones at younger and younger ages. In my personal experience I have seen a healthy vegan diet cure and extremely improve "incurable" diseases. Being a vegan is not the only answer to healthy living but it is one.

So, in the Vegan Soulfood Guide to the Galaxy I chose to focus on the soulfood aspect of cooking because vegetarian and especially vegan food has a stigma of being bland and dry. Vegan food can be tasty, simple and inexpensive. This guide also attempts to educate and help guide you through the maze of health information as well as make it practical to incorporate healthy choices into your life.

The **Nutrition and Shopping** sections are comprehensive guides to arm and educate you in this journey. You will receive many questions from your friends and family as you begin to change your eating habits. These sections were designed to help you get through the transition as easily and healthfully as possible. Being aware of what to buy, where to shop, where to get necessary nutrients and how to read labels are key things that can make or break the vegan experience.

The **Meat and Dairy** section attempts to expose what is going on in the meat, dairy and food processing industries and how the food these industries are producing is affecting our health.

The **Dining Out Guide** helps make this lifestyle realistic so that you can continue to enjoy dining out with your loved ones and still be satisfied without the simple task of choosing what to eat becoming an unmanageable, discouraging "big deal." The list of restaurants and suggested foods to order will help you have somewhere to begin.

There are **over sixty soulful recipes** to show that a vegan can be healthy and eat good food simultaneously—and not just rabbit food. It was very important to me that all the recipes were made with whole grains and natural sweeteners, excluding white flour, white sugar and white rice. Adding more whole grains and reducing the amount of processed foods extremely improves your health. Being a "junk food vegetarian" is not healthy and can lead to major health problems. There are also allergen guides in each recipe to help decipher if there is gluten or soy in the recipes.

As a bonus, there is also a DVD included entitled Pimp My Tofu that shows you how to prepare tofu with a soulful touch. This Tofu 101 crash course gives you the basics such as what tofu is, how to buy it, season it and make it taste like something your family will enjoy.

I hope you enjoy what's in store for you! Wherever you are in your eating choices there is something in this book for you. Be well, be healthy!

- Afya

FORWARD

photo by chester higgins

With diabetes, AIDS, high blood pressure, asthma, prostate cancer, fibroid tumors, obesity, hypertension and addiction to drugs, and yes, addiction to unhealthy food sweeping through our communities, like a plague, it's time for change. The "Fast Food Generation" is attached to the microwave and Corporate Kitchen chains. This generation eats meat from animals that have been fed growth hormones and antibiotics not intended for human consumption. Worse, this generation eats meat from animals that have been cloned! Eating such foods has caused detrimental blows to our bodies, minds and spirits. No wonder so many suffer everything from mood swings to cancer. We have lost control of our wellness. "The time for change is now."

Affordable healthcare is a topic most people in America hope change for the better. Among impoverished citizens, particularly in the African- American, Caribbean and Hispanic communities, good health has been spiraling swiftly downward; while the cost of insurance has been rising. Limited finances often limit access to the tools of wellness, such as wholesome foods, healthy living conditions and good medical care. In order for more people to enjoy wellness, it is time for change.

As a child of the 60s I witnessed the birth and rise of a multiplicity of transformation movements, the Black Power Movement, the Antiwar Movement, the Flower-Child, Free Love and Hippy Movements, to name a few. These movements sprang up on the college campuses and affected communities and politics throughout America. They inspired my personal change. Through the Vegetarian & Wellness Movement I liberated my inner-self from diseases brought on by the SAD (Standard American Diet) of low frequency foods. In that era of change, I changed how and what I ate. No more all-American meat and potatoes! I embraced Holistic Wellness and Purification. My reward was deliverance from chronic asthma, hay fever, arthritis, PMS and depression. Hallelujah! I healed myself.

And so it began. I healed myself and took a million people with me. I wrote: Heal Thyself for Health and Longevity, Sacred Woman: A Guide to Healing The Feminine Body, Mind and Spirit, and most recently, The City of Wellness: Restoring Your Health Through the 7 Kitchens of Consciousness. As a wellness-pioneer who has ushered a generation of people to take back control of their own health, I recognize The Vegan Soul Food Guide to the Galaxy as an amazing eye-opening, page-turner bound to renew this generation and generations to come. You are about to go on a transformation journey to a next-level galaxy of wellness. Liberation thru Purification.

Love,
Queen Afua

TABLE OF CONTENTS

Intro

Forward

VEGAN FAQ'S?   PG 16-23
    What Is A Vegan?   pg 16
    Types of Vegans   pg 16
    Why Vegan?   pg 18
    Health Advantages   pg 18-21
    The Need for A Guide   pg 21

THE MEAT AND DAIRY QUESTION   PG 26-33
    Politics of the Food Industry   pg 26
    Beef   pg 27
        Diseases: Colon Cancer,
        Heart Disease, High Cholesterol,
        High Blood Pressure   pg 27-28
        Growth Hormones/Antibiotics   pg 28-30
        Ecoli and Mad cow   pg 30
        Cloning   pg 30
    Chicken/Turkey   pg 31
    Pork   pg 31
    Fish/Seafood   pg 31-32
    Dairy   pg 32
        Lactose Intolerance   pg 33
        Casein/Asthma   pg 33

NUTRITION   PG 36-45
    Where to begin   pg 36
    Vegan Nutrients   pg 37
        EFA's   pg 38
        Protein   pg 38-41
        Iron   pg 41-42
        Zinc   pg 42
        Calcium   pg 42-43
        Vitamin D   pg 43-44
        Vitamin B12   pg 44
        Sprouting   pg 44-45

Let's Go Shopping .... PG 48-71

Where to Shop .... pg 48
    Health Food Stores .... pg 48
    Farmer's Markets .... pg 48
    Grocery Stores .... pg 49
    Food Co-op .... pg 49
    Urban Organic Farms .... pg 49
    Community Supported Agriculture .... pg 49
    Cultural Grocery Stores .... pg 50
    Home Gardens .... pg 50

Organic food .... pg 50-53
    Oganic Living .... pg 50
    What is Organic Food? .... pg 50
    Pesticides/Herbicides .... pg 50
    Genetically Modified Foods (GMO's) .... pg 51
    Biosolids (sewage sludge) .... pg 51
    Irradiation .... pg 52
    Our Environment .... pg 52-53
    Why is organic food so expensive? .... pg 53

Filling your basket .... pg 53
    Fruits/Vegetables .... pg 53
    Whole Grains .... pg 53-54
    Non whole grains- flour, bread and pasta ..... pg 54-56

Protein .... pg 56-58
    The Question of Soy .... pg 56-57
    Tofu, Edammame, Tempeh, TVP, Beans .... pg 57-58
    Nuts/Seeds .... pg 58
    Seitan .... pg 58

Fats and Oils .... pg 58-62
    Mono-, poly- and saturated fats, EFA's .... pg 59-60
    How oils are processed .... pg 60
    Unrefined, refined, trans fats .... pg 60
    and hydrogenated oils .... pg 60
    What oil should I be using? .... pg 61
    Olive, Sesame, Palm, Peanut, Coconut,
    Flax and Hemp oils .... pg 61-62

Natural Sweetener's .... pg 62-64
    Diabetes .... pg 62

Agave nectar, maple syrup, honey,
brown rice syrup, black strap molasses,
stevia, sucanat   pg 63
Boot-leg natural sweetener's   pg 64

Water, herbal tea, milks, juices and smoothies   pg 64-65

Sea Veggies   pg 65-67
Kombu, Spirulina, chlorella, nori, seamoss   pg 66

Fermented Foods   pg 67

Herbs, Spices and Condiments   pg 67-68

Reading Labels   pg 68-71
Top 10 Additives and Preservatives to Avoid   pg 69
High Fructose Corn Syrup   pg 69
Monosodium Glutamate (MSG)   pg 69
Hydrogenated/ Partially
hydrogenated oils   pg 70
Hidden Milk and Dairy   pg 70
Food Coloring   pg 70
Natural Flavors   pg 70
BHA/BHT   pg 71
Aspartame   pg 71
Sugar and Sweeteners   pg 71
Gelatin   pg 71
Caffeine   pg 71

DINING OUT/ MENU GUIDE   PG 74-79
Dining Out   pg 74
Restaurants/Traveling   pg 74-77

Foods to Limit or Avoid   pg 77-79
Processed Foods   pg 77
Caffeine   pg 78
Soda and juice drinks   pg 78
Microwave   pg 78
Fast Food   pg 78

RECIPES AND MORE!   PG 82-152
Breakfast   pg 82-87
Fresh Fruit Kebobs   pg 82

Hearty Breakfast Potatoes	pg 83
Satisfy My Soul Grits	pg 84
Sun-day grits	pg 84
Stacks (pancakes)	pg 85
Tasty Scrambled Tofu	pg 86
Tempeh Sauxsage	pg 87
Minute Spinach	pg 87
Soups	**pg 88-91**
Lemongrass Coconut Soup	pg 88
Vegetable Miso Soup	pg 89
Curry Lentil Soup	pg 90
Down Home Chili	pg 91
Salads	**pg 92-97**
Garvey Salad	pg 92
Kale Salad	pg 93
Sesame Tofu Salad	pg 94
Community Coleslaw	pg 95
Pasta-fari Salad	pg 96
My Mama's Potato Salad	pg 97
A Salad A day	pg 98
Main Dishes	**pg 99-110**
Savory Sauxsage Seitan	pg 99
Savory Brazilian Sauxsage	pg 100
Pepper Steak	pg 101
Buffalo Tofu	pg 102
Southern Fried Tofu	pg 103
Chimichanga	pg 104-105
Tofu-Tater Wrap	pg 106
Creole Red Beans and Rice	pg 107
Daal	pg 108
Sauxsage Pizza	pg 109
Crispy Fried Cauliflower	pg 110
Sides	**pg 111-130**
Veggies	**pg 111-124**
Al Greens	pg 111
Coconut Collards	pg 112
Crispy Collard Green Rolls	pg 113
Pz & Cz	pg 114
B-Sprouts	pg 114
Coup de Grille Veggies	pg 115

Gold Grilled Corn pg 116

Grains pg 125-130

Brown Pride Rice pg 125
Classic Corn on the Cob pg 117
Mouth Waterin' Butternut Squash pg 118
Cant' Believe This is Squash pg 119
Yams Sweet Yam pg 120
Mashem' Up pg 121
Oven Roasted Sweet Potato Fries pg 122
Brooklyn Fried Plantains pg 123
Sweet Baked Beans pg 124
Cinnamon Coconut Cous Cous pg 126
Fried Rice pg 127
Mo Millet pg 127
Wache pg 128
Cornbread Dressing pg 129
Mac-N-Cheez pg 130

Breads and Desserts PG 131-145

Breads pg 131-137

Country Corn Bread pg 128
Hush pups pg 132
East Indian Roti pg 133
Traditional Pizza Dough pg 134
NY (no yeast) Pizza Dough pg 135
Zulu Muffins pg 136
Nana Muffins pg 137

Desserts pg 138-145

Basic Pie Crust pg 138
Sweetie Pie pg 139
The Original "Crown Heights Apple Pie pg 140
Hood Rich Brownies pg 141
Carob Brownie Squares pg 142
Chocolate City Cookies pg 143
Rice Nut Krispies pg 144
Karamu Corn pg 145

Beverages pg 146-149

Spirulina Shake pg 146

Peach Cobbler Smoothie pg 146
Smoothie Guide pg 147
Green Goddess Smoothie pg 148
Hemp My Smoothie pg 148
Go Green Juice pg 149
Green Light Cocktail pg 150

Sauces and Dips **pg 150-151**
Good Ol' Guac pg 150
Motza Cheez Sauce pg 150
Mushroom Gravy pg 151

Cooking with Tofu pg 152
Cutting Tofu pg 153
Cooking with Whole Grains pg 154
Cooking with Beans pg 155

Tools You Need pg 156
Menu Planning pg 157-158
Shopping List pg 159-161
Substitution Basics pg 162
Glossary pg 163-164

ResouRces   PG 167-174

Resources pg 167-169
General References pg 169-174

About the Author
Ads
Index

CHAPTER 1
VEGAN FAQS

WHAT IS A VEGAN?

Vegetarianism has been around for thousands of years and is documented as being practiced by the ancient Egyptians and Ethiopians in Africa, Hindus in India, Buddhists in China and is even talked about in the Bible. Many of these vegetarian cultures were based on the health benefits of non-animal source diets while others were based on beliefs in reincarnation and karma (what goes around, comes around). Some cultures believe if you kill an animal for food you may be killing one of your ancestors. You wouldn't want anyone to kill you if you are reincarnated as a cow. In some cultures such as the Hindu, it was thought that eating meat would promote sloth (laziness) and ignorance as opposed to eating vegetables, which would promote a healthy body and a calm and peaceful spirit.

So what's the difference?

VEGETARIANS do not consume any meat, including but not limited to chicken, pork or fish, but they may eat eggs, milk, cheese or dairy.

VEGANS do not consume any animal products including but not limited to, meat, chicken, pork or fish, eggs, milk, cheese or dairy.

Just as there are many sects of religions and types of spirituality, the same holds true in the vegetarian world. There are types of vegetarians that eat eggs (ovo-vegetarian), types that each cheese and milk and no eggs (lacto-vegetarian) and types that eat eggs and milk (lacto-ovo-vegetarians). However, a **vegan** goes a little further and aside from not eating meat, **does not eat cheese, milk, eggs or dairy** and some do not eat **honey**. There hasn't been a 100 percent vegan society in recordable history so this concept is fairly new to human beings. Even ancient cultures that were primarily vegan would consume in very small amounts (less than 3 percent of their total diet) either some fish, insects or fermented dairy products.

Some people choose to become vegans because they believe that our bodies are not made to be able to digest and fully assimilate animal products and therefore, consuming them can contribute to chronic diseases and poor health. There are others who are vegan because of the fight for animal rights and against cruelty towards them. Others are vegans because they don't think that animals willingly give up their bodies or milk for anyone other than their own offspring.

What a vegan is has evolved and changed over the years. Personally, I do not like labels; I think they can be limiting and stifling. I will, however, attempt to explain and define the different types of vegans I've encountered as well as some eating disciplines that can sometimes be a little confusing within the vegan lifestyle. There are basic vegans, vegan activists, live foodists, fruitarians and macrobiotics.

Basic Vegans- Most of these vegans may have chosen to become vegan for health reasons. They may or may not be activists for animal rights. They do not eat meat, fish, poultry, pork, eggs, cheese, milk or dairy products. Some may choose to consume honey, wear leather and other animal products.

Vegan Activist- These vegans are usually animal rights activists. They make a conscious effort to avoid all forms of exploitation and cruelty to animals. They may also be a part of an organization that promotes and fights against animal cruelty. They do not eat meat, fish, poultry, pork, eggs, cheese, milk, dairy products or honey. They also do not wear leather or fur, use animal-based soaps or any products derived from or tested on animals.

 Live/Raw Foodist- These vegans consume mostly raw foods (no cooked foods) or foods that have not been heated over 118° F. They believe that the greater percentage of raw food within your eating habits, the healthier you are, and that raw food can heal and prevent disease. Raw foods also contain enzymes that help aid in the digestion and assimilation of nutrients. Their diet contains mostly raw fruits, vegetables, nuts and seeds. Some raw foodists eat raw meat and dairy products, but many are vegan. Some may choose to consume raw honey, as well as wear leather and other animal products.

 Fruititarian- Within the live foods community are fruititarians. These vegans don't eat anything that they have to harm its "creator" to eat. So (generally speaking) fruits are okay because the apple

tree is still standing when you eat the apple, but foods like carrots and greens are not okay, because you have pry up the whole carrot or green plant to eat it. Within this lifestyle, fruits are considered to be any fruit or "vegetable" with a seed, like cucumbers, tomatoes, and squash. Fruititarians

Children under three years old, and the elderly, have immature or low levels of the stomach acids that help break down live food, so their ability to digest raw foods is more difficult. Please consult a natural health practitioner to do this healthfully.

consume mostly raw fruits (no cooked foods) or foods that have not been heated over 118° F. They believe that the greater percentage of raw food in the diet, the healthier you are and that raw food can heal and prevent disease. Some may choose to consume nuts, seeds and raw honey, as well as wear leather and other animal products.

 Macrobiotics- These vegans live by a philosophy of balance (yin and yang) and living in harmony with nature while eating a simple, locally grown and mostly whole food diet. They also believe that the energy of food directly affects one's mental, emotional and

Fact: Donald Watson, in Europe, coined the term vegan in 1944

4 Types of Vegetarians

Lacto- (meaning milk) does not eat meat (ex. beef, poultry, fish, shellfish) or eggs, but eats dairy products (ex. cheese and ice cream).

Ovo- (meaning eggs) does not eat meat or dairy products but eats eggs.

Lacto-Ovo- does not eat meat, but eats dairy and eggs.

Pesco- does not eat meat, but eats eggs, dairy and fish. Some are Pesco-Vegans where they eat fish but not meat, dairy or eggs.

physical health. They exclude "nightshade" vegetables (white potatoes, green peppers, spinach, eggplant and tomatoes), refined sugar and most processed foods. Some are vegan and some are not.

> Nightshade vegetables contain a naturally occurring toxin called oxalic acid to prevent bugs from eating them. Tomatoes, eggplants, green peppers, spinach and potatoes (except sweet potatoes) are all in this group. Sensitivity to these foods may cause pain and swelling in people with arthritis as well as an over consumption may leech essential nutrients (like calcium) from your body.

Note: People who follow a macrobiotic diet must be cautious of a high sodium and caffeine intake.

Ital, Halal or Kosher? Have you ever been curious about these words and what they mean? Here are 3 eating disciplines based on spiritual beliefs you may encounter on your journey.

 Ital- Ital food is the approved food for people who adhere to the Rastafarian religion. Ital means pure, natural and clean. The laws are similar to the Leviticus and Deuteronomy books of the Bible. They do not eat shellfish, no fish larger than the palm of the hand, no chemicals and they avoid excess salt, alcohol or pharmaceutical drugs (herbs are not considered drugs). Not all Rasta's are vegan, but many are.

Halal- Halal is an Islamic law that regulates how meat is prepared.

Pork is forbidden and animals must be treated with a sense of respect. Animals eaten cannot be sick or already dead before slaughter. They have to be prayed over and all the blood must be drained out before slaughter. Halal does not mean vegan but vegetables and grains are considered halal if they are not cooked with meat or dairy products.

 Kosher- Kosher follows the Jewish laws about how food is prepared and eaten. Kosher is very similar to halal because the animal must be prayed over, cannot be sick or already dead at the time of slaughter, and all of the blood must be drained. Shellfish and pork are not permitted, and all animals must be treated somewhat humanely. The kosher diet also follows food combination laws whereby meat and dairy cannot be eaten together. Kosher does not mean vegan but fruit, vegetables, grains, spices and beans are considered kosher unless cooked with meat products.

WHY VEGAN?

Now that we have discussed what a vegan is, let's discuss why someone may want or choose to become vegan.

The leading causes of death in the U.S. are cancer, heart disease, diabetes, and obesity. Traditional soul food, poor diet, malnutrition, smoking and drinking cause the majority of these diseases. Luckily, all of these health problems can be prevented and probably cured on a healthy vegan diet. You don't have to be a vegan to be healthy but eating a 98% balanced vegan and organic diet is optimal for good health and longevity.

What are the Health advantages of a vegan diet?

Being a vegan has many advantages! Some of these advantages include improvement or

✳ VSG: KNOW YOUR HISTORY

Studies suggest that you can develop diseases, weaknesses and vulnerabilities based off your family health history (heredity). This means that if your mother or father has diabetes, you can become vulnerable to that disease as well. As a child you may suffer some symptoms from your family (such as asthma and allergies), but as you age it has been shown that you can reverse or change your chances of getting these diseases if you choose a healthy lifestyle.

Please place a check by a disease that you know someone in your family has or had, then write what their relationship is to you (mother, uncle, etc.) and check if they are still living. The purpose of the exercise is to show you what disease(s) you may be prone to based on heredity and to urge you to think about the quality of life you'd like to lead.

1. ____Diabetes   Who _____   living_____   deceased____

2. ____Heart attack   Who_____   living_____   deceased____

3. ____Stroke   Who_____   living_____   deceased____

4. ____Overweight   Who_____   living_____   deceased____

5. ____Cancer   Who_____   living_____   deceased____

6. ____High blood pressure Who_____   living_____   deceased____

7. ____Asthma   Who_____   living_____   deceased____

8. ____Kidney/liver problems Who_____ living_____   deceased____

total elimination of chronic diseases, improved energy and overall well being, weight maintenance, improved menstrual cycles as well as overall vitality and longevity.

Improved energy and overall wellbeing

The Idis (eye-dis) is a term used to describe the feeling of extreme fullness at the end of a meal. You feel bloated, sleepy and uncomfortable, but oooweee, that meal you ate was worth it! These feelings come from your body trying desperately to digest and break down all of the food you stuffed in it. Your body has a system in which it digests foods (carbs, proteins, fats). So if you eat a piece of chicken, french fries, apple pie and a soda, your body must decipher everything you have put in it, separate what should be digested first, then break it down. In turn you begin to feel tired because your energy is being focused on digesting these heavy foods. Introducing whole grains, fresh fruits and vegetable, nuts and beans will regulate and increase your energy and put less of a stress on your immune system, keeping you supplied with ample energy everyday.

Improvement or Total Elimination of Chronic Illnesses:

I suffered from asthma, allergies, irritable bowel syndrome and frequent colds my entire life, until I became a vegan. My mother also had asthma and was diagnosed with MS (multiple sclerosis). After eliminating toxins from her body through abstaining from cooked foods, consuming medicinal herbs and then adopting a healthy vegan diet, her asthma has disappeared and her MS has improved so much so that she no longer has to take MS medication. These are just two examples of the healing aspect of a vegan lifestyle, but there are many more. When someone is dealing with a serious disease, one therapy is to fast, cleanse and detoxify because your diet plays a key role in whether or not you contract diseases such as cancer, diabetes, heart disease, high blood pressure, obesity and more. Eliminating meat, dairy, soda, candy, sweets, poor quality oils, processed white sugar, white flour, and white rice, then incorporating whole grains, fresh fruits and vegetables, nuts, seeds and water helps your body begin its healing process.

Weight Loss/Weight Maintenance

Having a healthy balanced vegan diet (we will discuss later) enables you to maintain a comfortable weight. Initially you may lose weight once you change your eating habits, primarily due to detoxification, but also because your body will begin to find its ideal weight. Over time you will find what foods work best for you to keep your weight where you like it.

Regulated and Eased Menstrual Cycle

As a woman and a health counselor I can bear witness that many of my female clients' menstrual cycles have eased up. They experience milder cramps (or none at all), reduced blood flow and a reduction in PMS symptoms. Did you know that cows are injected with (and subsequently, dairy is laced with) growth hormones that attack and settle in women's reproductive organs and may show

✳ VSG: KNOWLEDGE IS POWER!

Raising Vegan Children

Around the country there have been cases of vegan children who are malnourished. These children are either dying or being taken away from their parents by local authorities. Then the parents are getting put in jail for life, supposedly, for neglecting their kids. Some vegan parents are targeted and receive heavy sentences because they are going against the status quo when in reality they are just unaware of how to raise vegan children. Children have different nutritional needs and making sure that they are getting enough of the correct nutrients is very important. Vegan or not, children are picky eaters and it can be a challenge to fulfill their daily required nutrient intake. Breastfeeding is also a must for vegan mothers. Even if you work, find a way to pump and give your baby the nutrients they need. As of 2009, there are no 100 percent vegan baby formulas. If there is just no possible way for you to breastfeed, organic goat milk formulas may be better than cow's milk. There is no excuse for ignorance. If you choose this lifestyle, you must educate yourself!!!

Beware of the Starch!

Starch-a-tarian- I first heard the term "starchatarian" from Queen Afua, author of *Heal Thyself*, *Sacred Woman* and *City of Wellness*. She defines a starchatarian as a "vegetarian" that rarely eats vegetables and mostly eats, white bread, white pasta, french fries, sweets, white rice, white sugar and veggie chunks (TVP). Don't be a starchatarian!

up as fibroids, cysts and endometriosis? Processed foods, meat and dairy can also congest your intestines causing constipation, which can worsen cramps.

Longevity and Vitality

Studies have shown that vegetarians have a lower incidence of cancer, heart disease, high blood pressure, obesity, and diabetes. This is primarily due to their food choices. The longest living people in the world have a whole food, organic, and 97 percent vegan diet (3 percent comes from seafood, insects or fermented goat or dairy products).

The Environment

By becoming a vegan or significantly reducing your meat intake, you are helping to protect the environment. The waste of land, water and energy it takes to raise, feed and produce livestock is contributing to global warming, soil destruction and water depletion (less available drinking water). At the same time, the antibiotics and growth hormone laced manure from farm animals is seeping into the earth's soils and water. This spreads toxins to us through the water we drink and seafood we eat, which destroys animals and throws off the balance of nature.

WHAT DOES SOUL HAVE TO DO WITH IT?

Cooking and preparing food is a way we express our love for our family and friends. Food is what brings many of us together during holidays and weekends. Soul food in general is comfort food prepared and eaten in most cultures of people of color. More specifically, in the United States it has been coined as food from the African cultures influence on the cuisine of America that grew out of slavery.

The history of soul food in America came out of slavery where the master would give the enslaved captives the scraps or the least desirable parts of the animal for their food. That usually consisted of, chittlins (pig intestine), fat back (pig back), tripe (cow stomach), liver and gizzards (organs of the animal), pickled pigs feet, cow tongue and ribs. Europeans also brought crops from Africa like sweet potatoes and wheat. We used our African and Indigenous knowledge of spices and herbs to make whatever we were given tasty and edible. Eating pork and drinking cow milk was not prevalent in the traditional African diet. These foods, and more, have become part of the reason for the rampant and high rate of disease in people of color.

THE NEED FOR A GUIDE

Changing your eating habits is more than just changing the food that you eat; it's also *changing your lifestyle*. Even though changing your diet can be an exciting time in your life it can also be a bit stressful and frustrating. You will no longer just pick up anything to eat or drink without thinking about it, and you will have to find new restaurants and places to eat and shop. You will also go through withdrawal from your body detoxing itself from meat, dairy and junk food. Your friends may not understand you; your mate may have serious problems and complaints as well. Dealing with constant questions from family and friends, along with doubt and sometimes-negative comments can also add to your stress. This guide is a needed resource that you will turn to again and again to reconfirm and strengthen your decision to improve your health.

Another need for this guide is that there are vegans and vegetarians who are not healthy. A lot of vegans/vegetarians think that because they are not eating animal products they are healthy, but their diet consists of mostly processed soy products, white breads and pastries, white rice, white sugar, very few vegetables and poor oils. This type of diet can lead to diabetes, yeast infections, chronic fatigue syndrome, weight gain, malnutrition and cancer. The goal of this guide is to help you to be confident about living a healthy lifestyle through wise food choices, basic nutritional understanding, and healthful recipes. The recipes in this book attempt to utilize a mix of whole foods, soy products, and balanced meals so they are nutritious as well as delicious. ✦

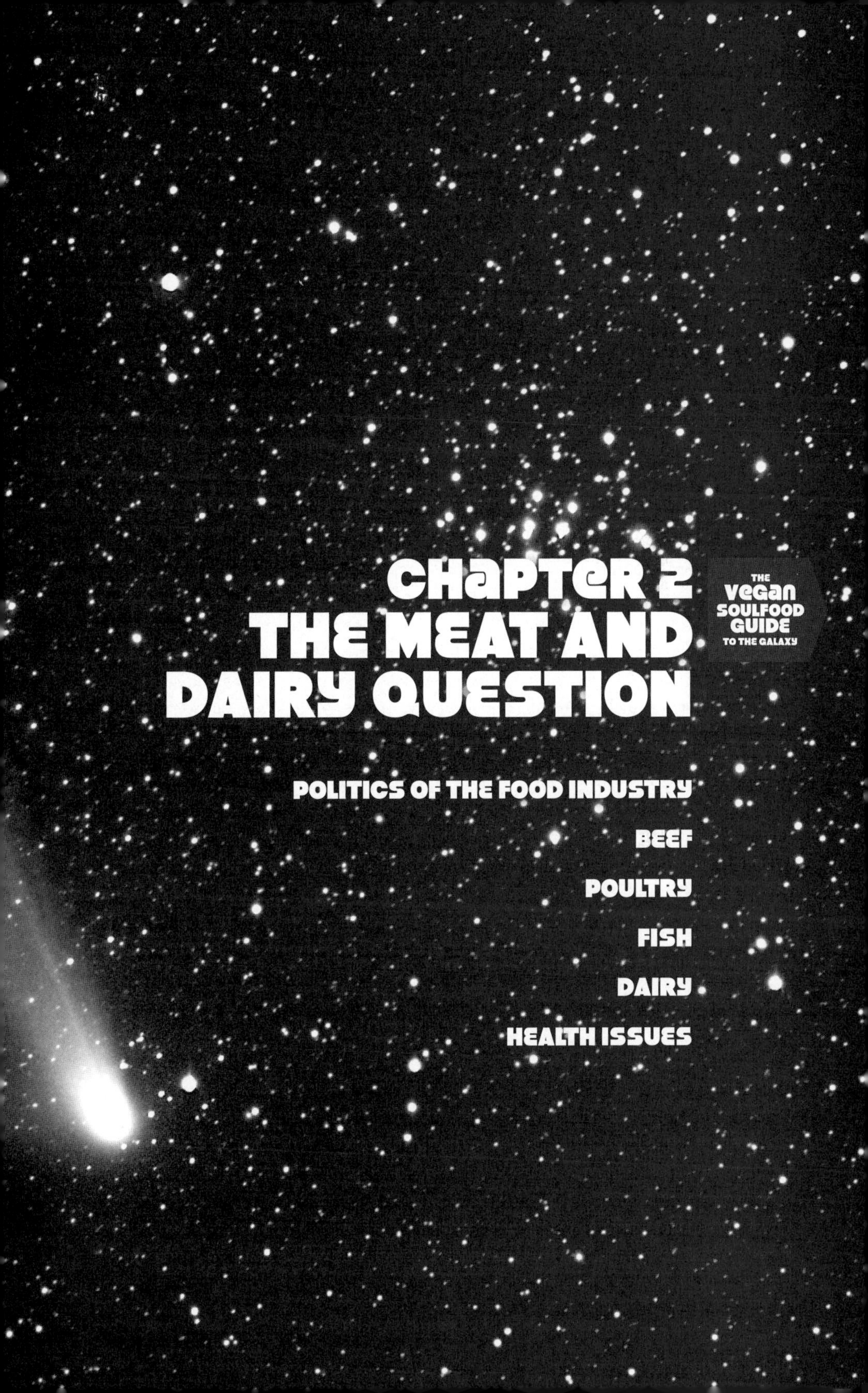

CHAPTER 2
THE MEAT AND DAIRY QUESTION

THE VEGAN SOULFOOD GUIDE TO THE GALAXY

POLITICS OF THE FOOD INDUSTRY

BEEF

POULTRY

FISH

DAIRY

HEALTH ISSUES

"I can't give up my meat"

"That soy stuff is made out of cardboard"

"So what's wrong with meat?"

These are comments that I hear all the time. There really is a lot of confusion about what's healthy, what's balanced and what we should eat. In general, most scientists and doctor's agree that a diet high in animal meat and low in fiber can and will lead to heart disease, high cholesterol, high blood pressure and cancer.

POLITICS OF THE FOOD INDUSTRY

Today in the U.S. most people eat the Standard American Diet (SAD), which mostly consists of fast food, cheeseburgers, ice cream, snack cakes, potato chips, hot dogs, pizza, fried chicken, soda, french fries and candy. The SAD that we are so familiar with today is really new in the evolution of the human being and our history of food consumption. After WWII (around 1945) there was a shift from small farmers and local food to the industrialization of the food industry which produced canned, boxed, processed and chemically altered food. Large factories and farms had machinery that allowed for more food to be grown and harvested as well as added chemicals to enhance food's color, flavor and shelf life. This increase in food production had an impact on international shipping, which ultimately led to more money. As business grew, the "old way" of life began to change. Factories, companies, businesses, grocery stores and restaurants started popping up all over the country. With the invention of this new food and distribution industry, hundreds of thousands of jobs were created. This growth in the economy (the consumption of goods and services in a country) was part of forming the concept of "Big Business". The more profit large corporations made, the more the United States economy grew, as did their world economic power.

The food industry is a large part of the financial support of America. Billions of dollars and hundreds of thousands of jobs are supported by the meat, dairy, chemical, and food processing industries. These industries partner with policy makers, politicians and governmental groups like the USDA (United States Department of Agriculture), FDA (Food and Drug Administration) and the EPA (Environmental Protection Agency) to promote nutrition based on their products. We, as consumers, get advice from these agencies about our nutritional needs in the form of the basic four food groups, or the food guides. These guides decide what is promoted on television, sold in grocery stores and served in schools, hospitals and prisons.

Commercials and advertising made by and paid for by these same food processing corporations, focus on the psychology of people and how to have their products in people's minds all the time. These ads help to boost the featured company's sales regardless of the foods nutritional value or its possibly harmful ingredients. Corporations also market their products to specific age groups and genders using clowns, catchy songs, and sexual fantasies. These commercials and jingles have worked their way into the majority of the food choices we make on a daily basis. In the U.S. there are 80 million people with cardiovascular disease, 40 million people who are obese, 20.8 million with diabetes and1.5 million with cancer. Many of these diseases can be tremendously reduced or avoided just by changing our eating habits and

Meat Eater or Vegetarian?

There are meat eaters and vegetarians in the animal kingdom. Most of us have seen video footage of lions tearing through the flesh of zebras or giraffes eating leaves off trees. There are different theories about if human beings have the appropriate intestinal system to be able to digest meat. As humans, unlike animals, we have the ability to choose if we want to eat meat or not. Let's look at the differences in natural meat eating animals and naturally vegetarian animals..

Carnivore - Carnivores are primarily meat eaters. They have long, sharp incisors (cutting) and canine (stabbing) teeth to be able to tear through the flesh of other live animals and consume the meat uncooked. Carnivores also have strong stomach acids and enzymes to digest high amounts of fat, cholesterol and protein and to kill parasites and worms found in raw animal meat. Their intestines are only six times their body length and do not have the enzymes to digest plant protein. Types of carnivorous animals are lions, cheetahs, wolves and eagles.

Herbivore - Herbivores are plant eaters. They need less protein than natural meat eaters. Herbivores require a lot of energy to stay alive so they eat all day long. They have large stomachs to be able to take in lots of food. Their digestive system is full of bacteria and enzymes that can help break down plant cellulose (what we call fiber or roughage). Herbivores intestines are 10 to 12 times the length of their body. Humans intestines are 10 to 11 times their body length. Types of herbivorous animals are horses, cows, elephants and sheep.

Omnivore - Omnivores have intestinal systems that can digest plant and animal protein [after the age of four, some lose the ability to digest lactose (milk sugar)]. Unlike herbivores, omnivores do not have the ability to digest cellulose, but it is used in their body to help aid in digestion. Humans also cannot digest cellulose. They have a mix of incisors (cutting), canine (cutting), and molars (grinding) teeth. The length of their intestines is 4 to 6 times their body length. Types of omnivores are bears, chickens, chimpanzees and pigs.

food choices. The sad part about it is, the food industry and the government are more interested in profits rather than our health. So for this reason, it's time to take our health into our own hands with education, discipline and wise food choices.

The Beef with Beef

Beef has gotten its fair share of press over the last few decades because of its high cholesterol and saturated fat levels. The over consumption of red meat has been linked to diseases such as colon cancer, heart disease, high blood pressure, and increased cholesterol.

Colon Cancer

According to the Journal of the American Medical Association, people who eat large amounts of meat double their risk of colon cancer. This is partially due to the amount of time that red meat stays in your intestines, coupled with a lack of exercise, lack of water consumption and a diet low in fruits and vegetables which contain the necessary fiber to move food along quickly. It takes fruits and vegetables 4-12 hours (fruit being the fastest) to digest, as opposed to red meat which takes 2-3 days. The longer the meat sits in your body the more bacteria and free radicals (molecules that can cause premature aging) build up. That build-up can lead to cysts, constipation, bowel troubles, polyps and cancer.

Heart Disease

Consuming large amounts of red meat, which contains saturated fat and cholesterol, has been linked to strokes, heart attacks and atherosclerosis (clogged arteries). Eating more protein and saturated fat than your body can metabolize (breakdown and use as energy) and excrete increases your chance of developing heart disease.

High Cholesterol

Cholesterol is a fatty wax type substance that is made by the liver of mammals. Your body naturally makes cholesterol to form cells in your body, aid in digesting fat, and to make hormones and vitamin D. Consuming too much fat and cholesterol can clog your arteries, cause heart disease and heart attacks. Meat and dairy products are the only food sources of cholesterol. There is no cholesterol in fruits, veggies, beans or whole grains.

High Blood Pressure (Hypertension)

Your blood pressure is the force of blood against the walls of your blood vessels. High blood pressure, or hypertension, is when your heart has to work harder to force blood through the rest of your body. High blood pressure is also associated with obesity, diabetes, heart attacks, kidney and heart failure. Raised cholesterol levels and clogged and hardened arteries can lead to high blood pressure.

Growth Hormones/Antibiotics

According to the European Union's Scientific Committee on Veterinary Measures Relating to Public Health, there are six growth hormones given to cows to promote faster growth and more milk production. The growth hormone rBGH (recumbent bovine growth hormone) is one of those

Oprah's got BEEF!

In April of 1996, Oprah Winfrey did a show about dangerous foods. One of her guest speakers, Howard Lyman, talked about mad cow disease. He was discussing the details of cattle being fed other ground up cows, which caused mad cow disease. His information led Oprah to say that she would not eat a hamburger again.

This statement prompted the Texas beef industry to sue Oprah for defamatory remarks under the "Veggie Libel" bill. This actual bill claims that "because food products constitute a large portion of the state's economy… [Farmer's have] a legal cause of action…to recover damages for the disparagement [comments that cast a doubt about the safety] of any perishable agricultural food product."

This bill helps to discourage free speech about the harmful practices of the food industry. Even if you prove your health claims, you are being hassled and forced to pay money for your court fees. Fortunately, Oprah was not found liable for her comments; she has made a big step for free speech!

* VSG: EATING TOO MUCH FAT, PROTEIN AND CHOLESTEROL?

Eating the SAD (Standard American Diet) makes it easy to surpass the RDA's (Recommended Daily Allowance) of saturated fat, protein and cholesterol. High protein, low fiber diets can put a strain on the liver and kidneys and contribute to an excess loss of calcium. Children are at the greatest risk. Childhood obesity, diabetes and cancer are increasing every year.

RDA's for:

Cholesterol

Adults- less than 300 mg* per day

Children- less than 150 mg per day

Protein

Adults-25-65 g* per day

Children and teens 14-45 g per day

Saturated Fat

Adults and Teens- 20 g per day

Children (6 to 8 yrs)- 4.8 -6 grams per day

Children (9 to 12 yrs)- 6 - 7.5 grams per day

The chart below shows the amount of saturated fat, cholesterol and protein in different types of meat and dairy products.

Food	Amount	Sat fat	Cholesterol	Protein
Grilled chicken breast roasted	1 cup	3.06 g	118 mg	41.72 g
Fried chicken wing	6	11.6 g	156 mg	50.16 g
T bone steak	6 oz	5.87 g	116 mg	21.26 g
1 small hamburger	3 oz	5.98 g	71 mg	19.93 g
Fish stick, frozen	6	4.63 g	54 mg	18.54 g
Grilled Atlantic Salmon	3 oz	1.06 g	60 mg	21.62 g
Fried catfish	6 oz	2.8 g	69 mg	30.76 g
Scrambled eggs	2 large	4.48 g	430 mg	13.52 g
Shrimp	8 large	.128 g	86 mg	9.2 g
Milk	12 oz	4.6 g	30 mg	12.07 g
Cheddar cheese, diced	1 cup	23.8 g	119 mg	28.14 g
Chocolate ice cream	1 cup	8.97 g	44 mg	5.02 g
Bacon	4 oz	14.8 g	126.4 mg	42.8 g
Dominoes pepperoni pizza	3 slices	15.3 g	79.2 mg	41.7 g

*There are 16 ounces in a pound and 8 ounces in one cup.

*g = grams   *mg = milligrams

hormones. The use of the genetically engineered growth hormone rBGH was approved by the FDA without proper testing. This use of hormones in the U.S. beef industry has caused Europe to ban the importation of U.S. and Canadian beef to Europe. That decision has cost Europe $120 million a year in sanctions since 1997. The beef that Europe banned, but America still eats, contains hormones that can possibly lead to prostate, breast and colon cancer, as well as menstrual problems and early sexual development in children. Cows on these hormones get mastitis (infection and inflammation of the utters), internal bleeding and sickness. These health problems contribute to the use of antibiotics in cows, which is transferred to humans when they eat it. Consuming large amounts of antibiotics from animals makes humans immune to the treatment of antibiotics, as well as reduces the amount of healthy bacteria in the intestines, which makes the human body prone to infection.

Ecoli and Mad Cow Disease

According to the Center for Disease Control (CDC), e-coli bacteria causes at least 73,000 infections, 60 deaths and thousands of pounds of meat to be recalled each year. Crowded conditions, filth and feces in the meat processing plant can contaminate cows with the bacteria when meat is cut or ground. Feeding cows strictly grains and synthetic feed instead of their natural greens/grass diet also makes them susceptible to disease and infection. When they are sick, antibiotics are used to treat them, which transfer to humans. There are also the remaining visibly sick "downer" animals that are so sick they cannot stand up. These animals are ground up and used as feed for chickens, pigs, farmed fish and other livestock.

Mad cow disease or Bovine Spongiform Encephalopathy (BSE), is caused by cows being fed ground up cow, pig and chicken parts as well as sheep brains. In 1997 the FDA prohibited the use of most animal parts in cow and goat feed, except milk products, blood products, gelatin, pure pork and horse protein. Feeding cow products and meat to cows that are herbivores, is turning them into carnivores and cannibals! No wonder the cows go mad!

CLONED MEAT

Cloned meat is a growing bio (life) science in the food industry. The food industry (and government) is changing the natural structure of animals and making them into a new species. Genetically engineered and cloned animals are designed to have desirable traits, such as disease resistance, leaner meat and larger animals without the use of growth hormones. Studies show that the majority of clones have heart disease, respiratory failure, malformations, defects and large offspring syndrome (LOS) where cows are born much larger than normal and they must be delivered by cesarean section. Clones are also born with weakened immune systems that leave them more susceptible to infection, which equals more antibiotics.

Scientists and doctors who oppose the rush to release this new technology on the public say that

> ## What is Cloning?
> **According to the Center For Food Safety, Cloning or Somatic Cell Nuclear Transfer (SCNT):**
>
> Involves fusing the genetic material of a cell from an existing animal into an egg removed from another animal. Once the egg is fertilized in the laboratory, it is implanted into a "host mother." Then a clone is born.

there are no studies on the health effects of full grown animals. Even if they appear to be healthy, there may be some underlying disease or genetic mutation. The FDA calls this risk a "subtle hazard."

The FDA's approval of cloned meat was all over the news in early 2007. One of the biggest issues was the labeling of meat products that have been made from cloned animals. The FDA has decided that there is no need to label meat and milk products made from cloned animals, so that means they may already be on the shelves.

Chicken & Turkey Facts

Poultry (chicken and turkey) consumption has increased with the health claims to reduce red meat. But just like beef, chicken is prone to disease and harmful bacteria. According to the Center for Disease Control (CDC), 40,000 cases of salmonella poisoning happens every year with 600 fatalities and 2500 cases of listeriosis (bacteria infection), causing 500 deaths. The symptoms of these two bacterial infections are similar to the flu, so many cases of salmonella poisoning may go undetected.

Antibiotics are given to poultry to kill bacteria and as growth promoters. The growth promoting aspect makes chickens able to lay more eggs, grow faster and larger. These antibiotics contain the poison arsenic that can cause cancer, heart disease and diabetes. Antibiotics can also reduce the good bacteria in your intestines that help to break down nutrients and build your immune system. Eggs are high in cholesterol and are also susceptible to salmonella, and everything that chickens are susceptible to.

Pig Facts

Whether it's because of religious reasons or because you just believe it's a filthy animal, the pig is a controversial animal, and most people know at least one person that does not eat pork. Pig is outlawed in Islam, with orthodox Jews, Seventh Day Adventists and even in the bible. Pigs are prone to having parasites and tape worms which can transfer to humans if the meat is not cooked well enough. Pork is also treated with nitrates/nitrites (an additive) in the curing process to help kill bacteria and add a pink color to the meat. Nitrites turn into a toxic form once it enters the body that may lead to cancer. Pigs are also given a muscle relaxant type drug in their feed, which is used as a growth enhancer to increase the leanness in meat. This feed causes "downer" animals that are unable to get up and walk.

Fish and Seafood

Fish has been promoted as a "wonder" food because it's rich in Omega-3 and Omega-6 fatty acids that help to reduce cholesterol. Fish and seafood has been the main source of meat for many cultures for thousands of years. Unfortunately, as technology has grown, large levels of environmental toxins such as oil leaks, mercury, dioxins and PCB's from industrial, nuclear and chemical waste (see page 50 about organic food), has polluted the majority of water on earth. The oceans, waterways and animals that live in them have been turned into a toxic mess. Mercury is one of the most commonly known pollutants of fish and is a naturally occurring element in nature that is used in the medical, dental, and chemical industries. Methyl mercury is an altered form of mercury found in fish. When we digest this type of mercury it can cause mouth sores, nausea, vomiting, headaches, vision and hearing loss. Pregnant women are advised to reduce or eliminate fish because mercury may cause mental retardation, cerebral palsy and seizures in embryos and newborns.

Farmed Fish

Farmed salmon are another topic amongst themselves. They are farmed similar to livestock, given antibiotics, and are fed the ground up unsaleable parts of animals (hoofs, skin). Because salmon must also eat other fish for their fat and protein to gain weight, concentrated fish oil is added to their feed. Fish oil is highly contaminated with PCB's, a toxic pollutant (see page 164 for info on PCB's). In 2004, a study was released in the scientific research journal, Science, confirming that the high level of contaminates in farmed Atlantic salmon means it should not be consumed more than once a month.

Organic meat and organic dairy products do not have growth hormones or antibiotics, and are not fed any other animal products. Organically farmed animals are fed their natural diet, but they are still high in saturated fat and cholesterol.

The researchers' analysis showed that consumers should not eat farmed fish from Scotland, Norway and eastern Canada more than three times a year; farmed fish from Maine, western Canada and Washington state, no more than three to six times a year; and farmed fish from Chile, no more than about six times a year. Wild chum salmon can be consumed safely, as often as once a week. Pink salmon, Sockeye and Coho can be eaten about twice a month and Chinook just under once a month.

Dairy - Milk and Milk Products

Like most kids, cheese was one of my favorite foods as a child. Mac & cheese, pizza with extra cheese, nachos and cheeseburgers made up at least 70 percent

of my diet. I also suffered from extremely bad asthma and allergies as a child, and did not receive substantial relief until I stopped eating dairy. Deciding not to eat dairy products is one of the main things that separates a vegan from a vegetarian. Just think about it, we are the only mammals on this earth that willingly drinks the milk of another animal. Most animals drink their mother's milk up until a certain age and then stop. Cow milk is high in fat, cholesterol and growth hormones and has been linked to asthma, allergies, fibroids, osteoporosis, SIDS, arthritis and cancer.

Lactose Intolerance - Lactose Intolerance is an allergy to the sugar (lactose) in animal milk. Ninety-five percent of the people of color in the world are lactose intolerant. Our bodies have the ability to digest our mother's milk until the age of four. After that, we begin to lose the enzyme lactase (a substance that helps the body digest milk sugar) and it becomes more difficult to digest milk or milk products. Common symptoms of lactose intolerance are: diarrhea, nausea, abdominal cramps, bloating, gas and irritable bowel syndrome.

Casein and Asthma- The protein in dairy is called casein. The protein content in cow's milk is designed to turn a 60 pound calf into a 300 pound cow. These large protein particles can be too overwhelming for your body to digest which can lead to mucus buildup in the lungs, asthma, chronic allergies, hives and rashes, constipation, irritable bowel disease, circulation problems, heart disease, weight gain and can stress the liver causing liver problems. ✦

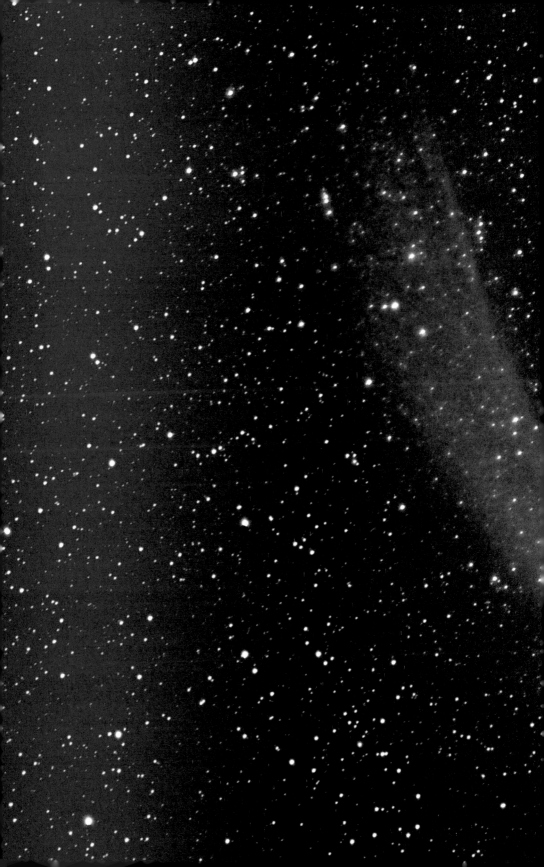

CHAPTER 3
NUTRITION

NECESSARY NUTRIENTS
AND THEIR SOURCES

WHERE TO BEGIN

If you have decided to become a vegan you probably want to know where to begin, right? Eliminating meat and dairy can be a little scary because you want to make sure you are getting all of the nutrients you need. Many people have given up chicken, but not fish or dairy; some have given up dairy but not fish. Wherever you are, be patient with yourself and take it one day at a time. These steps below can help you get started and stay healthy.

Get Healthy!

SEVEN STEPS TO BECOMING A VEGAN

1. Take one type of food out of your diet every two weeks. Begin by taking one food out, whether it's cheese, chicken, soda or milk. Decide and stick with it. Also be aware of reading your labels; you'd be surprised how much food contains milk, cheese and eggs. (See page 70.)

2. Add one new food to your diet every week. I see many people who take everything out of their diets, but don't add anything new, which can lead to malnutrition and fatigue. Add a new vegetable, grain or fruit that you have never had before. Either find a recipe that sounds good or try it at a restaurant.

3. Eat from the color spectrum. Eat foods that are red, yellow, green, orange, brown and white- daily. This should ensure that you are getting balanced nutrients. Also eat a green vegetable everyday. If you are not eating any, start off with one. If you are eating at least one, then add two and so on.

4. Eat raw fruits and vegetables everyday. Make a salad, eat some fruit, and drink a smoothie or a fresh veggie juice EVERYDAY! Raw fruits and veggies are ignored in our lifestyles, but are so vital.

5. Limit processed foods. When eliminating meat; we have a tendency to gravitate towards, bread, rice, pasta, and sweets because these foods are quick, convenient, and familiar to us. When you begin to eat all of these foods you will gain weight. I call this the "Veggie 15," the extra pounds you gain when trying to figure out this new lifestyle. Using these steps will help to eliminate this problem.

6. Read and research. Information is key! Take time out each week to learn about nutrition, read a vegetarian magazine, or try a new recipe.

7. Be patient with yourself.

You will go through withdrawal, crave meat, have headaches and even become irritable. You will also eat things without being aware that it has meat, milk or cheese in it. Don't beat yourself up, worry or give up. A new lifestyle takes time and effort. YOU CAN DO IT!

VEGAN NUTRIENTS

People frequently ask me "if you're a vegan, is it possible to get all of your nutrients?" Of course it is! In a perfect world, if you are eating a well balanced

diet you will get all the nutrients you need. Now we live in a world where most of the soil has been denatured based off poor farming practices so you cannot be sure if the soil is nutrient rich, unless you are growing your own. So just for safety purposes, taking a whole food multi-vitamin at least three times per week, along with balanced eating habits, should ensure that you get all of your nutrients. Regular check-ups should provide the diagnosis you need to adjust your program.

There are a whole host of vitamins, minerals and nutrients that we need on a daily basis but I have only touched on a few that have come into question in vegan malnutrition. If you are vegan and feel fatigued, malnourished, anemic or are having any chronic health problems it may mean that you maybe missing one or a few of these following nutrients.

Recommended Daily Allowance (RDA)					
NUTRIENTS	MEN (25-71+)	WOMEN (25-71+)	CHILDREN (0-10)	TEEN (11-24)	PREGNANT /LACTATING
CALCIUM	1000-1200 mg	1000-1200 mg	400-800 mg	1200 mg	1200mg
VITAMIN D	200-600 IU	200-600 IU	200 IU	200 IU	200 IU
ZINC	11 mg	8 mg	2-5 mg	8-9 mg	11-13 mg
VITAMIN B12	2.4 mcg	2.4 mcg	.4-1.2 mcg	1.8-2.4 mcg	2.6-2.8 mcg
IRON	8 mg	8-18 mg	7-10 mg	11-15 mg	10-27 mg
PROTEIN	30-55 g	25-45 g	11-20 g	25-45 g	35-70 g
EFA'S*	16-19 g	12-13 g	5-11 g	11-18 g	14 g
Omega 3 + Omega 6 fatty acids					

Essential Fatty Acids

(EFA's A.K.A Vitamin F)- are basic components of fats and oils that are used as energy in your cells. They are essential because your body does not make them; you have to get them from the foods you eat. EFA's come in two families (Omega 3 and Omega 6). Your body needs a balance of both of these types of oils to promote healthy nerves, blood, arteries, skin, hair and reduce cholesterol. Types of EFA's are flax and hemp seeds.

Vegan EFA Food Sources		
	OMEGA 3	OMEGA 6
Avocado- 1 medium =	.22 g	3.39 g
Walnuts (raw)- ½ cup =	5.3 g	22.2 g
Almonds (whole raw)- 1 cup =	.28 g	8.73 g
Flax seed (ground)- ¼ cup =	6.38 g	1.65 g
Olive oil- ¼ cup =	.4 g	5.27 g
Hemp seeds - 2 tbsp =	2 g	5 g
Spirulina- 1 tbsp =	7.78 mg	11.75 mg
Kidney beans =	.297 g	.185 g
Romaine lettuce (l head) =	.707 g	.294 g
Oranges (1 med) =	.012 g	.032 g
Navy beans (1 cup) =	.213 g	.162 g

EFA Deficiency can lead to: fatigue, dry and/or itchy skin, brittle hair and nails, constipation, depression, frequent colds, slow or stunted growth, poor concentration, hair loss, lack of physical endurance and joint pain. A healthy diet should consist of one gram of Omega-3 fatty acids to four grams of Omega-6 fatty acids. So for every one gram of Omega 3 you consume you should also consume 4 grams of Omega 6. Too much omega-6, particularly in relation to omega-3 fatty acids can contribute to long-term diseases, such as heart disease, cancer, asthma, arthritis, and depression. (See page 60 for Omega 6 consumption)

Protein-Protein is an essential nutrient that is contained in every part of the body: the skin, hair, nails, muscles, organs and bones. Its primary function is to regulate growth hormones, and also build, repair and maintain tissues, organs and muscles in your body.

Vegetarian Sources of Protein©

Vegetables (1 cup cooked)	Protein (g)
Split peas	16.35g
Chlorella (1 1/2 tbsp)	14.9 g
Baked potato (7 oz)	8.7g
Green peas, frozen	8.24g
Spinach	5.97g
Artichokes	5.85g
Brussels sprouts	5.64g
Asparagus	5.31g
Mixed vegetables, frozen	5.21g
Broccoli	4.65g
Beet Greens	3.7g
Beets	2.86g
Parsnips	2.06g
Tomatoes	1.53g
Green cabbage	1.53g
Peppers	1.25g
Red cabbage, raw	0.97g
Leeks	0.84g

†Daily Protein Requirements	
Children 1–4 years	11–16g*
Children 5–18 years	20–45g*
Adult women	25–45g*
Adult men	30–55g*

Dried Fruit (pieces)	Protein(g)
Raisins, (1 cup)	4.67g
Dried apricots, (5)	1.19g
Figs, (2)	1.16g
Prunes, (5)	1.1g
Dates, (5)	0.8g
Dried apples, (5)	0.3g

Fruit (1 medium fruit unless stated)	Protein(g)
Papaya	1.85g
Melon (1 cup)	1.41g
Orange	1.23g
Banana	1.22g
Mango	1.06g
Grapes (1 cup)	1.06g
Blackberries (1 cup)	1.04g
Blueberries (1 cup)	0.97g
Cherries, sweet, raw (10)	0.82g
Grapefruit, white (1/2)	0.81g
Kiwi fruit	0.75g
Grapefruit, pink (1/2)	0.68g
Peach	0.69g
Pear	0.61g
Apricot	0.49g
Apple	0.26g

g= grams

Beans (1 cup)

Beans (1 cup)	Protein (g)
Tempeh	31g
Soy beans	28.23g
Tofu	22.1g
White beans	19.02g
Lentils, cooked	17.86g
Navy beans	15.83g
Black beans	15.24g
Great Northern beans	14.74g
Baked beans	12.17g
Pinto beans	14.04g
Refried beans	13.83g
Kidney beans	13.44g
Lima beans	11.97g
Chick peas/garbanzo	11.88g
Black-eyed/cowpeas	5.23g
Mung beans, cooked	2.52g
Green snap beans	1.55g

Protein Equivalents

1 cup soymilk = 1 cup 2% milk

1/2 cup peanuts = small salmon filet

1 cup lentil soup = small chicken breast

3/4 cup green peas = 1 scrambled egg

1 cup tofu = 1 small hamburger

1 cup cous cous = 1 small steak

Your body can only digest 20 to 30 grams of protein every 2-3 hours. Any extra protein is stored as fat.

Grains (1 cup)

Grains (1 cup)	Protein (g)
Couscous	22.07g
Barley	19.82g
Bulgur	17.21g
Wheat flour, whole grain	16.44g
Oat bran	16.26g
Buckwheat flour	15.14g
Quinoa	11g
Cornmeal	11.7g
Buckwheat, groats, roasted	5.68g
Brown rice	5g

5-18*† grams of protein per meal is all your body needs.

Nuts/Seeds (1 oz)

Nuts/Seeds (1 oz)	Protein (g)
Pumpkin seeds	9.35g
Squash seeds	9.35g
Peanuts	6.71g
Almonds	6.03g
Sunflower seeds	5.48g
Walnuts	4.32g
Cashew Nuts	4.34g
Hazel Nuts	4.24g
Brazil Nuts	4.07g
Pecans	2.6g
Sesame seeds, 1 TBS.	2.55g
Macadamia Nuts	2.21g
Alfalfa seeds, 1 cup	1.32g

* Requirements may vary depending on your age, weight and level of activity
† Based off 3 meals per day.

Vegan sources of iron
left going clockwise: chickpeas,
lentils and spelt flour

Protein deficiency can lead to- slow growth in children, frequent infections, wounds that won't heal, fatigue, weakness and severe edema (swelling and fluid retention).

Iron- Iron is an essential mineral that helps in carrying oxygen to your cells. Iron is necessary for energy, strong blood and a healthy immune system. Blanching or lightly cooking vegetables as well as soaking seeds and nuts help to increase the digestibility and absorption of iron.

Vegan Iron Sources

Pumpkin seeds ½ cup = 14.97 mg

Spelt flour 1 cup = 9.4 mg

Soybeans- 1 cup cooked = 8.8 mg

White beans- 1 cup canned = 7.8 mg

Lentils- 1 cup cooked = 6.6 mg

Spinach – 1 cup cooked from fresh = 6.4 mg

Tofu ½ cup= 6 mg

Kidney beans 1 cup cooked= 5.2 mg

Chickpeas 1 cup cooked = 4.8 mg

Black beans 1 cup= 3.6 mg

Blackstrap molasses- 1 tbsp = 3.5 mg

Carob powder- 1 cup = 3.3 mg

Potato 1 large = 3.2 mg

Almonds- ½ cup, whole= 3.07 mg

Tahini ½ cup = 2.51 mg

Black eyed peas 1 cup cooked = 2.3 mg

Tomato puree ½ cup = 2.2

Lima beans ½ cup cooked= 2.2 mg

Navy beans ½ cup cooked = 2.1 mg

Refried beans ½ cup = 2.1 mg

Collard greens- 1 cup (cooked) = 2 mg

Tomato paste ¼ cup = 2.0 mg

Dates- 5 = 1.1 mg

Beets- 1 cup = 1.09 mg

Kale- ½ cup (cooked) = .58 g

Spirulina- 1 tbsp = .53 mg

Iron deficiency can lead to- anemia, fatigue, low birth weight, brittle hair, hair loss, inflamed mouth sores, obesity, difficulty maintaining body temperature. It can also delay normal activity and movement in infants and slow thinking, processing and social development skills.

Vegan sources of zinc
left going clockwise: oats, quinoa, chick peas, lentils, pumpkin seeds

Zinc is found in every part of the body. It helps in the healing of wounds, the growth and health of reproductive organs, prostate gland functioning, and adequate semen. Men need more zinc than women for the health of their reproductive organs.

Vegan Zinc Food Sources

Quinoa 1 cup = 5.61 mg

Pumpkin seeds- ½ cup = 5.14 mg

Whole wheat flour 1 cup = 3.52 mg

Chickpeas ¾ cup = 2.8 mg

Lentils 1 cup = 2.51 mg

Oatmeal 1 cup = 2.49 mg

Pecans- ½ cup = 2.24 mg

Wild rice = 2.2 mg

Corn meal 1 cup = 2 mg

Sunflower seeds- ¼ cup = 1.8 mg

Black eyed peas- ½ cup = 1.8 mg

Lima beans 1 cup = 1.79 mg

Hemp seeds 3tbsp = 2 mg

Spinach 1 cup = 1.37 mg

Brown rice 1 cup = 1.23 mg

Whole wheat bread 2 slices = 1 mg

Baked beans ½ cup = 1 mg

Shitake mushrooms- 4 = .96 mg

Mushroom Portobello- 1 cup = .52 mg

A deficiency of zinc results from inadequate intake of zinc, or inadequate absorption of zinc into the body. Signs of zinc deficiency include eczema, hair loss (alopecia), fatigue, diarrhea, white spots in your nails, decreased growth rate and mental development in children.

Calcium is necessary for forming and maintaining strong bones and teeth, blood clotting, muscle growth and the prevention of muscle cramps.

Collard Greens are a great vegan source of Calcium

Vegan Calcium Food Sources

Tofu ½ cup = 400 mg

Collard greens 1 cup cooked = 356 mg

Black strap molasses 2 tbsp = 344 mg

Spinach 1 cup cooked = 292 mg

Edammame 1 cup cooked = 260 mg

Tahini, raw ¼ cup = 238 mg

Almonds raw ½ cup = 177.5 mg

Carob- ½ cup = 179 mg

Almond butter ¼ cup = 169 mg

Flax seed, ground ½ cup = 144 mg

Kale 1 cup raw = 135 mg

Turnip greens ½ cup cooked = 124 mg

White beans ½ cup cooked = 96 mg

Okra ½ cup cooked = 88 mg

Oats- 1 cup = 84 mg

Spelt 1 cup = 77.6 mg

Broccoli 1 cup = 43 mg

Kelp 1 tbsp = 42 mg

Spirulina 1 tbsp = 15 mg

A deficiency in calcium may show up as: eczema, aching joints, nervousness, arm and leg numbness, tooth decay, the rickets, muscle spasms, nose bleeds and twitching.

Shiitake mushrooms

Vitamin D

This vitamin helps the absorption of calcium and phosphorus which helps to strengthen bones and teeth. The most reliable source for Vitamin D is exposure to the sun; 20 minutes a day is the minimum amount for people of color (15 minutes for Caucasians). If you live in the colder regions, make sure you get some sun every day. Shiitake mushrooms are one of the few known vegan food sources with this vitamin.

Vegan Vitamin D Food Sources

Shiitake mushrooms 4 pieces- 249 IU

Fortified non-dairy milk- amount varies for each brand

It has been said that you can find Vitamin D in these following foods as well, but they are not considered reliable sources, so get some sun!!

Oatmeal

Sweet potatoes

Alfalfa

Dandelion

A Word About Spinach.

Spinach is a perfect example of the need to rotate your foods. Spinach, as well as tomatoes, green bell peppers and eggplant are known as a nightshade vegetables. These foods are healthy but an over abundance may cause problems with arthritis and take calcium out of your body.

Nettle
Parsley
Dark green leafy vegetables
Chlorella (see page 66)

A deficiency in Vitamin D can lead to: The most common Vitamin D deficiency disease is the rickets, which is a bone disease that happens in children causing bowlegs and bone deformities. Vitamin D deficiency can also lead to nose bleeds, slow healing and muscle cramps.

Chewing Your food.

Chewing your food well helps to improve digestion and release the nutrients in foods. Chewing each mouthful 20-50 times helps you to relax, enjoy your food and manage your weight.

Vitamin B12

Vitamin B12 is necessary for the forming of red blood cells, the maintenance of the nervous system, and growth and development in children.

B12 is one of the most controversial issues for the vegan lifestyle. Conventionally, people will get their B12 from vegetarian animals that eat from the ground, freshly picked vegetables that may contain traces from the soil, seaweed or their bodies automatically make it. Since we rarely pick fresh vegetables without washing them, there are only a couple of food sources to get it from. Studies have been done on the digestibility of B12 from seaweed sources but the amounts and usability of it from seaweed has not been "proven." Taking a multi-vitamin or B12 supplement at least three-four times per week or consuming B12 fortified foods can ensure you are getting what you need.

Vegan Vitamin B12 Food Sources
Nutritional yeast (Red Star brand)- 2 tbsp = 8 mcg
Chlorella – 1 tsp = .06 mg
Spirulina – 1 tsp= 2 mcg

Amounts in these sources vary:
*Fortified cereal, nuts & non-dairy milks
*Multi vitamins
*Soil

A deficiency in Vitamin B12 causes anemia, paleness, weakness, mouth sores, fatigue, depression and disorders of the nervous system.

Sprouting

Sprouting is the practice of soaking and draining seeds, grains and beans until they germinate and begin to sprout. Sprouting grains increases the content of protein, fat, certain essential amino acids, water, B vitamins the activity of enzymes and the digestibility of the starch. It also decreases phytates as well as enzyme and protease inhibitors. When grains, seeds and beans are dry, most of their enzymes are inactive. That's what allows them to be able to last for years with out going bad. But these inhibitors could cause a depletion in minerals in the body such as calcium and contribute to digestive issues. This is why beans, nuts, seeds and grains should be soaked, fermented or sprouted to reduce the effects. ✦

THE INGREDIENTS
BEANS

Bottom left going clockwise: black beans, Yellow split peas, Red beans, Green lentils, Black beans, Canalloni (white) beans, Red lentils and Black eyed peas. See page 57

NUTS
See page 58

SQUASH
Top left going clockwise:
1. Turban, 2. Kabocha, 3. Sweet dumpling, 4. Pumpkin, 5. Acorn, 6. Butternut and 7. Delicata.

SEA VEGETABLES
Top left going clockwise: Spirulina, Nori, Wakame, Dulse flakes, Kelp, Seamoss.
See page 65

SEEDS

Top to bottom: Hemp seeds, Flax seeds, Sesame seeds, Sunflower seeds and Pumpkin seeds.
See page 57

NATURAL SWEETENERS

Top left going clockwise: Maple syrup, Agave, Mollases, Brown rice syrup, Honey, and Sucanat (center).
See page 62

SHADY MAPLE FARMS

CERTIFIED ORGANIC
PURE
MAPLE SYRUP
U.S. GRADE B
32 FL. OZ. (1 Quart) (946mL)

SNACKS Top tray: vegan rippled potato chips, popcorn, vegan bbq chips. Top left: salsa. Top right: hummus . Front- left going clockwise: pistachios, carrot chips, pretzel sticks, romaine lettuce, whole grain crackers, blue corn chips, tofu cream cheese (center).

SEITAN Seitan- freshly made seitan (sauxsage). Seitain is a sausage substitute that can be fried, baked and grilled. See page 99

PROTEIN SOURCES

Left going clockwise: Miso, Potatoes, Yellow split peas, Red lentils, Pumpkin seeds, Quinoa (center).
See page 39

EFA'S (ESSENTIAL FATTY ACIDS) SOURCES

Left going clockwise: Romaine lettuce, Almonds, Avocado, Flax seeds, Spirulina and Walnuts. Center-hemp seeds.
See page 38

NON-DAIRY CHEESE

Top left going clockwise: Nutritional yeast (see page 68), rice "cheddar" slices and soy block "cheese".

WHOLE GRAINS

Top left going
clockwise: Barley,
Quinoa, Kamut, Oats,
Wild rice, Brown rice,
Popcorn, Bulgar wheat,
Millet, and Black rice.
See page 53

MEAT SUBSTITUTES Top left going clockwise: Tofu, Veggie "chicken", Veggie burgers, Tempeh, Veggie hot dogs, Textured vegetable protein (TVP) and Veggie fish. See page 57

PROCESSED WHOLE GRAINS Top left going clockwise: Veggie pasta, Cous cous, and Whole wheat bread. **Middle left going right:** Whole grain spaghetti, Corn thins, Wheat free waffles, Spelt pretzels. **Bottom left going right:** Fruit sweetened Corn flakes, Whole wheat pita, Blue corn chips, Whole grain crackers, Corn and Spinach tortillas.

CHAPTER 4
LET'S GO
SHOPPING

WHERE TO SHOP

ORGANIC FOODS

WHAT FOODS TO BUY

READING LABELS

WHERE TO SHOP

As you begin to eat healthier you also want to be able to afford your food. For a while you may have to shop around to find what stores have the best prices. I know I can get almond milk for $1.99 at the health food store, but the grocery store might sell it for $3.29. If the store with the cheaper prices is farther than your normal grocery store, consider being prepared to buy in bulk so you won't have to come back to that store more than once or twice a month. If you buy mostly whole foods like fruits, veggies, whole grains, nuts/seeds, beans, tofu or tempeh, your bill should be very reasonable. If you cannot afford to buy all organic, buy as much as you can. If you cannot afford to buy organic at all, still purchase mostly whole foods.

Health Food Stores

A health food store is a grocery store that specializes in natural and organic food. These stores can range from a full grocery store to just mostly vitamins and a few boxed and canned foods. Everything in a health food store is not necessarily "healthy" or vegan. They may sell organic meat, dairy and eggs. Some processed foods in the health food stores can be filled with white flour, white sugar, harmful additives and genetically modified ingredients. Be sure to read your labels!

Buying from bulk bins is less expensive than buying a pre-packaged item because you are not paying for the packaging process. Be sure to only buy bulk from a store that has a high turnover rate. Health food stores that do not have a large clientele may not change their bins often enough, leaving the food denatured and stale. Unfortunately, health food stores can be very expensive but there are some ingredients that you can only get there, or on the Internet. I have tried to limit the recipe ingredients in this guide so that the majority of them can be found at a regular grocery store.

Please do not confuse a health food store with a supplement store like GNC or The Vitamin Shoppe. A health food store usually has at least some produce, frozen, boxed and canned goods as well as vitamins and supplements.

Farmers Markets

Farmers markets are a wonderful way to find organic and locally grown produce where the farmers may take better care of their land and products with a minimal use of pesticides for a decent price. Based on the harvest availability, farmers markets also help you to eat seasonally to vary your diet and keep your body in tune with nature. Some cities have a market that you can shop at everyday and other cities have market's that are only open for business once or twice a week.

Grocery Stores

Many grocery stores have a natural food section, or are beginning to carry natural food because of the growing demand. The natural food section usually sells tofu, soymilk, organic produce and a few healthy alternatives. The good thing about these stores is that they have sales and discount cards. The down side is that if you can not find an item in the natural food section, you may not be able to do all of your shopping in one store.

Food Co-Op

A food co-op is a health food store that is co-operatively owned and operated by its members. Co-ops are great because you usually get food at a discounted price. Some co-ops are set up where if you work there once or twice a month you'll get a large discount. Others, you may pay a yearly fee to be a member and receive special savings throughout the year.

Urban Organic Farms

Urban organic farms are popping up all over the country. They are usually run by concerned citizens with farming experience that serve the community with fresh organic food grown on small plots of land. They have seasonal foods available and you can usually be a member and pick up food when it's harvested. If you live by a traditional farm, take a family trip and pick your own fruits and veggies!

Community Supported Agriculture (CSA)

Community Supported Agriculture consists of a community of individuals who pledge support to a farm operation. The growers and consumers provide support with the growing and running of the farm as well as share in the risks and benefits of food production. When you become a member of a CSA, you're purchasing a "share" of the food produced. Sometimes boxes of food can be delivered to your home or picked up in a common location. Most CSAs have a variety of payment plans to enable members flexibility in paying for their shares. A CSA season typically runs from June through November. However, some farmers also offer winter shares.

✳ VSG: Eating Seasonally and Locally

Eating seasonally means to eat the foods that naturally grow in that season (spring, summer, fall, winter). Eating locally is buying produce that is grown in your regional area. Eating seasonally and locally helps to build your immune system and keep you in tune with nature. These foods have the necessary nutrients your body needs at that time of year to acclimate your body to the weather conditions, keep your body in balance and strengthen your immune system. Having your own garden or going to your local farmers market can keep you aware of what's available in your area.

Cultural Grocery Stores

Asian, Hispanic and Caribbean grocery stores have a wide array of unique and delicious foods. Many of them sell vegetarian products, oils, spices, seaweeds and snacks that cannot be found in grocery or health foods stores. They can also be very reasonable priced.

Home Gardens

With the growth of the organic food industry, there is also a growth in the corporate control over the way foods are grown. We want to believe that all foods grown organically are truly organic but that may not be the case. With larger companies gaining more control over the industry organic farming is becoming more about paper work than an actual love for pure food. Not to say that there are not reputable farms out there but they are becoming targets for corporate take-overs. The change in the industry coupled with the rise in food costs has sparked many people to have their own gardens. Planting foods that you purchase on a regular basis not only makes sure that your food is organic; it also helps to save money. Planting vegetables or herbs in large tubs on your balcony or having a full garden in your yard all helps you to increase your nutrient intake and save money.

ORGANIC LIVING

I have been asked many times "why should I buy organic? Aren't fresh vegetables just fresh vegetables?" I wish that was the case. I used to say that if you don't buy anything that is in a box, can, or package, you would be okay. Unfortunately however, there is no list of ingredients for the mix of hormones, herbicides, pesticides, and toxic ingredients attached to a tomato or apple. Organic food used to be the only type of food we ate until the invention of harsh chemicals that were a result of the war industry and the invention of genetic modification.

What is organic food?

Organic food is grown without synthetic or harmful pesticides, herbicides, artificial fertilizers and the seeds have not been genetically modified. Processed organic foods use organic food ingredients and do not use any artificial additives, preservatives or irradiation. Farmers and producers are said to be thoroughly inspected to make sure they are following the rules.

Pesticides/Herbicides

Pesticides are used to kill bugs and insects that can damage crops and herbicides are used to kill weeds that can hinder the growth of crops. The modern use of pesticides and herbicides are a spin off from the production of germ warfare agents such as nerve gas (organophosphates) that the Nazi Party used in Germany to exterminate people, and the herbicides (Agent Orange) that the U.S. used in Vietnam to kill plants that were camouflage for the Vietnamese. Certain types of pesticides like DDT and PCB's were banned in the 70's, but are still showing up today in animals and their food products, our water and fish supply, as well as our bodies.

According to the United States Environmental Protection Agency (EPA):

The health effects of pesticides depend on the type of pesticide. Some, such as the organophosphates…[they] affect the nervous system (delayed motor skills in children). Others may irritate the skin or eyes. Some pesticides may be carcinogens (cancer causing). Others may affect the hormone, immune, reproductive (low birth weight, low sperm count and infertility) or endocrine (affecting normal growth and development) system in the body.

The harmful effects of dioxins (similar to Agent Orange) are:

Short-term: The EPA has found dioxin to potentially cause the following health effects when people are exposed to it at levels above the permitted amount for relatively short periods of time: liver damage, weight loss, wasting (destruction) of glands important to the body's immune system.

Long-term: Dioxin has the potential to cause the following effects from a lifetime exposure at levels above the minimal allowable: a variety of reproductive effects, from reduced fertility to birth defects and cancer.

Even though these risks exist from the use of pesticides, the EPA, FDA and USDA still allows them to be sprayed on our food.

Genetically Modified Foods (GMO's)

Biotechnology, or genetically modified organisms (food) is where the DNA or original structure of a food has been changed in some way that does not occur naturally. GM foods are supposedly produced to increase the nutritional value (amount of vitamins and minerals) in food and to protect crops from insects and viruses. Modifications may happen by adding the gene of a fish to a tomato so it can be weather resistant or have a longer shelf life. Or a seed can be genetically modified to have an insecticide in it so that fewer pesticides have to be sprayed on the plants. Corn, soy, cotton, potatoes and canola are the most common GM foods. They are used in making sweeteners (high fructose corn syrup), foodstuffs, flour, and oils (soy, canola or corn oil). The safety of GM foods is still in question but we are still being forced to eat them. If you are not eating organic food you are more than likely eating GM foods.

I Am Legend

Will Smith's movie "I Am Legend" briefly touched on the idea of gene transfer. The "cure" for cancer was a genetically modified measles virus.

The main concerns of genetically engineered foods are:

1. *Allergies-* the change in genes could cause an increase in allergies in humans.

2. *Gene transfer-* the new genes in the food can transfer to the genes or DNA in humans and mutate (change) it in some way possibly causing disease of the intestinal tract, cancer or worse.

3. *Out crossing-* is when the GM foods are made for animal feed or alternative energy sources but are not fit for human consumption. When the GM foods cross with traditional foods the newly formed gene is consumed by humans. These mutated genes can possibly lead to health problems.

4. *Welfare of animals and insects*- Some GM foods have a gene that kills insects; insects that are harmful to the plants and possibly helpful ones like bees.

Biosolids

Biosolids, otherwise known as sewage sludge, is used as a fertilizer to "rebuild and nourish" the soils of fruit and vegetable crops. Biosolids are the leftover solids from water treatment plants and began being used in the early 1990's. In theory, these biosolids would be the perfect way to fertilize the soil - kind of like compost. The issue is that chemicals, drugs, cleaning fluids, lawn fertilizer, heavy metals, lead, mercury, arsenic and basically anything that goes down the drain is being spread all over non-organic fruits, vegetables, whole grains, corn and soy. The EPA allows a certain amount of these toxins to legally be dumped onto the soil. There is a filtering process of the solids but it does not fully remove the industrial chemicals or medical and human waste that stays in the sludge. In turn, the sludge is affecting our water supply and may cause Hepatitis B, salmonella poisoning, cancer, and diabetes.

Irradiated foods

Irradiation is a form of radiation used in the food industry to increase the shelf-life of food, inhibit mold growth, as well as to kill insects, parasites and bacteria that may cause food borne diseases such as e-coli and salmonella. Even though irradiation is being used, there are still 73,000 cases of e-coli, 40,000 cases of salmonella, and 2500 cases of listeria (bacteria) poisoning every year, and that is only the cases that are reported. The food industry is currently pushing for irradiated foods to be labeled as "cold or electronically pasteurized" where customers will be unaware of this type of processing.

Irradiation comes from sources such as:
1. Nuclear waste
2. Radiation similar to what is used in cancer treatments
3. X-rays similar to what is used in doctors' or dentists' offices

The FDA and USDA say that irradiation poses no harmful effects to the human body, but studies show otherwise. According to the Center for Disease Control (CDC), the level of radiation used for meat is about 7 million times more than a single X-ray. It may be difficult to see the harmful effects of irradiation in some foods like a piece of chicken, but it's much easier to see the effects in foods, such as live oysters who are killed from irradiation, or eggs who's whites become more liquid and do not work well in recipes. Doctors and scientists who oppose irradiation report that this type of food processing can cause cancer, heart disease, mutations, stillbirths and severe vitamin and mineral reduction.

U.S. food regulations allow the irradiation of wheat and wheat powder, white potatoes, many spices, dry vegetable seasonings, fresh shell eggs, and fresh produce, fresh meat and poultry, including whole or cut up birds, skinless poultry, pork chops, roasts, stew meat, liver, hamburgers, ground meat, and ground poultry.

Our environment- organic farming does not release toxins and chemicals into the soil or water, which is healthier for the wildlife, the longevity and nutrients of the soil, and ultimately our health.

Why is organic and health food so expensive?

Let's be real, organic food is usually more expensive than conventionally grown food. Food pricing is a deep and intricate political agenda that goes all the way to the top. According to the FAO (Food and Agricultural Organization, a section of the United Nations) organic food is more expensive because there is less of a demand and that organic food costs more to grow. In actuality it only costs a farmer 10% more to raise or grow something organically. Large industrialized farms are subsidized by the government, which lowers their expenses. Non-organic processed foods also use cheap ingredients, made in a lab or factory that is either non-perishable or has an extremely long shelf-life, opposed to fresh food that is not meant to be edible for two years, ya dig?

FILLING YOUR BASKET

Shopping for your healthier lifestyle can be fun and frustrating at the same time. It's fun to try new foods but with the cost of food today, who wants to buy food, just to find out it doesn't taste good? Starting with more familiar whole foods like grains, fruits, vegetables and beans makes the process much easier.

Fresh Fruits and Vegetables

As stated earlier, fresh fruits and vegetables should be a large portion of your lifestyle. Fill your basket with an array of colors and textures. Attempt to have a green vegetable for every meal and purchase enough fruit to have as a snack and for smoothies. Fill 'er up!

Grains

Grains are a type of carbohydrate that serves as a source of energy in your body. There are many types of whole grains and rice to choose from.

Whole Grains

Adding whole grains to your daily food intake can make such a difference in your life. They are high in B vitamins, fiber and protein. Choosing whole grains instead of processed white grains can help you to lose weight, eat less, control your cravings, lower your insulin, give you more energy and help you to be more focused. When whole grains (complex carbohydrates) are eaten, they

✳ VSG: FRUIT/ VEGETABLE SPRAYS

Fruit and vegetable sprays can be helpful in removing waxes and some of the pesticides on the skin of produce. It may not remove everything, but it helps. You can also clean them by soaking them in a little vinegar for about 10 seconds and then rinsing.

break down into complex sugars, unlike white rice that converts into simple sugars. Complex carbohydrates, such as whole grains, digest at a much slower rate than simple ones. This slowed down process allows your blood sugar, as well as your energy, to remain stable and consistent throughout the day.

Types of whole grains are: Whole grain rice (brown, black, red, jasmine and wild rice), oats, quinoa, dried corn, millet, barley, wheat, spelt, amaranth, teff and buckwheat.

Quinoa- pronounced (keen-wah) is an ancient grain that has been used for 6,000 years by the Incan people in South America. It has the highest amount of protein of all grains.

Millet- has been used in Africa since 7000 BC. It's high in protein and B vitamins.

Gluten free grains: rice, millet, quinoa, teff, wild rice amaranth and corn

Wild rice- is indigenous to the Ojibwa and Sioux people. It is thought to be over 12,000 years old.

Kamut- is an ancient Egyptian grain that's over 3,000 years old. It is similar to wheat but is higher in protein and nutrients.

Non-whole grains

Foods made with whole grains are not the same as whole grains. They are processed foods made from whole grains. They are healthier for you than white flour products and have nutrients, but they are still processed and if eaten in excess, can cause weight gain and health issues.

White Rice

Brown rice has the outer hull removed from the grain, but the bran and germ remains. White rice is milled brown rice where the bran and germ have been removed and then polished. What remains is a shiny white grain of rice that cooks fast and has a long shelf life but has lost much of its nutritional value. It contains less fiber, zinc, magnesium and B vitamins than brown rice. White rice has added nutrients that are sprayed on to replace the nutrients lost in the milling process.

Flour

Flour is a powder made from ground up grains, corn, seeds, or beans. Wheat flour is one of the most popular flours used in the U.S. It's used in everything from bread, packaged foods, pastas, cereals and gravy. While whole-wheat flour can be nutritious, conventional wheat flour, or white flour can be very harmful to your health.

What is white flour?

White flour is the main type of flour used today in processed foods. White flour is a wheat plant with the outer layer (bran) and inner kernel (germ) removed and then bleached. What that means is the majority of vitamins, minerals and fiber of the plant has been removed. What this processed form of food does is raise your insulin level, similar to white sugar. White flour takes nutrients out of your body, such as calcium, in order to digest it. It can also cause weight gain by depriving your body of nutrients it is looking for, thereby forcing you to eat more to fulfill the nutrients your body is missing and craving.

Unbleached flour- is processed the same as white flour where the bran and germ are removed, therefore leaving it with a lack of nutrients except it has not gone through the bleaching process.

Whole-wheat flour- is made from the entire grain and is high in protein and B vitamins. The wheat that we know today is a hybrid of original grain, so it is not as digestible as other whole grains. Many people are allergic or sensitive to the protein in wheat (gluten). Symptoms of wheat sensitivity (gluten intolerance) may be bloating, eczema and yeast problems. If you don't have problems with wheat, feel free to use it. Whole-wheat flour can be found in most grocery stores.

Spelt flour- Spelt is an ancient grain that has been used since 6000 BC in Africa. It is high in protein, manganese and B vitamins.

Corn meal, rice, oat, millet, chickpea, and soy flour are other forms of whole grain flours.

Bread

I love bread, but the yeast does not agree with my body, as is the case with many women's bodies. Luckily there are many different types of breads available now so no matter what your allergies or yeast issues are, you should be able to find bread you can eat. Whole grain breads are healthier than white bread because they are closer to a whole food.

Grits- yellow grits are considered a whole grain. White grits are similar to white rice.

While reading labels, if it says wheat flour instead of whole wheat flour, its really white flour.

Yeast bread- is the common bread that you see on the shelf. Active yeast helps bread to rise and is what gives bread the soft consistency that we love. Read the labels because many contain high fructose corn syrup, sugar and milk.

Some people have issues with yeast-based products (like myself) and have recurrent yeast problems or excess build up of mucus. Reducing or eliminating yeast products helps to reduce and eliminate those issues.

Gluten free and yeast free bread have become an alternative for those who are sensitive to gluten or have yeast disorders. Both of these breads are usually harder than yeast breads and taste the best when toasted. It is difficult though to find a gluten free, yeast free bread that tastes good.

Sprouted grains- sprouting is a way to soak beans, grains and seeds to enhance their enzymes, vitamins, minerals and digestibility. These grains can be made into bread and are easy to find at health food stores and grocery stores usually in the freezer section.

Pasta

There are many different varieties of pasta. Whole wheat, spelt, rice, quinoa, corn and cous cous pastas can be found in most grocery stores around the country. When purchasing pasta, look for the word "whole" so that you know you are getting a whole grain product and not white flour. Make sure you read the cooking directions because some pastas only take a few minutes to cook. Non-wheat pasta can easily break up or get mushy, so after draining, immediately run it under cold water to stop the cooking process.

> **Cous cous** is thought to be a whole grain but is actually pasta. Buy whole wheat cous cous so you are getting a whole grain pasta.

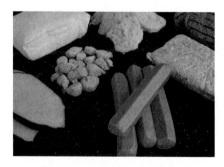

Protein

The question of soy

There is a lot of controversy about the safety of eating soy. But it's really not a question of if soy is safe; it is the type of soy that you eat and the process that it goes through. Soy contains chemicals in them called trypsin inhibitors and phytates. These chemicals can cause digestive issues and a decrease in nutrients in the body. Fermenting and sprouting soy helps to decrease these inhibitors to allow your body to digest soy safely. Also, non-organic soybeans are usually genetically modified and heavily sprayed with pesticides. The soy industry is expanding and now soy is showing up in cereals, energy bars, breads, soups and gravies in all forms like, soy oil, soy protein isolate and hydrolyzed vegetable protein. These types of soy are extremely processed and an over consumption may cause health problems. Soy can also be an allergen. Some people are born allergic to the protein in soy and some develop an allergy to it because of eating too much of it. A soy allergy can manifest as eczema, bloating and constipation.

Even though we may want to give up or reduce our meat consumption, we are literally addicted to it. Eating meat the majority of your life, as well as TV and the media promoting it to you all day every day, you crave the texture and taste. Because we have grown up in the processed food era, we may gravitate more to foods that look and taste like meat. Food companies know this and make foods that look and taste like meat to exploit our addiction. But over-processed food, vegan or not, is not a whole food and is a foreign substance to your body. Over consumption of processed soy can contribute to cancer, thyroid problems, weight gain, bloating, excess mucus and food allergies. I know these foods are quick, easy, and taste good, but please be aware of how much you are consuming. Organic tempeh, miso, and sprouted tofu are the best choices for soy intake.

How much is too much?

Veggie versions of burgers, chicken, fish, bacon, etc., help people who are just beginning to transition their diets and are having meat cravings until their pallets have gotten used to the new foods. Eating these foods for breakfast, lunch and dinner is too much. Mix up your protein sources with beans, seitan, quinoa, and veggies. Also switch up your milk choices. Soymilk is easy to find but too much soy can be mucus forming so try almond, rice, hemp, coconut or oat milks. The longer you are a vegan the less you should be eating highly processed soy foods. Eat them no more than two to three times per week.

Tofu (toe-foo) is made from soybeans. The beans are boiled, ground up and solidified. There are a few different textures based off of the amount of water added to it. It comes in silken, soft, firm, and extra firm. Silken and soft are best used for blended ingredients, cakes, pies, and puddings. Firm and extra firm are good for slicing, baking, sautéing, and grilling. Tofu has more flavor if it is marinated first for at least 30 minutes to overnight. I have been a vegan so long that I rarely marinate tofu and have found a few tricks to add flavor as I am cooking. Some people squeeze the water out of tofu before using it, but I usually don't unless I froze it first. Tofu can also be frozen and thawed to give it more of a meatier, firmer texture.

Sprouted Tofu- sprouted tofu is made from soybeans that have been soaked and sprouted. The sprouting helps to increase digestibility and reduce the phytates that can lead to health disorders. It's higher in protein, fat and calcium than regular tofu. It's still not acceptable for those allergic to soy but it is a better choice than regular tofu. Sprouted soy may be hard to find so call around or look on the internet.

Edammame (ed-a-ma-may)- are whole soybeans that are a great snack with sea salt and soy sauce.

Tempeh (tem- pay) is fermented soybeans and one of the best forms of soy. It's high in protein and has a sweet nutty flavor and can be fried, baked, sautéed or grilled. Tempeh has a very unique flavor and should always be marinated or highly seasoned.

Textured Vegetable Protein (TVP)/ Soy Protein Isolate (SPI): TVP comes in many tastes, sizes and textures. There is SPI veggie fish, chicken, ham, beef, seafood, cold cuts, bacon, sausage and more. They are a great substitute for everything you would use meat for. They are also good to bring to family gatherings for the more skeptical friends and relatives. There is also TVP, also called "chunks." This type of soy comes in "chicken," "beef" or ground. It has to be rehydrated with hot water and seasoned before cooking. Hydrolyzed vegetable protein can come from, soy, wheat or corn. If it's not organic, it is probably genetically modified. There is a lot of controversy about the use and health effects of SPI and TVP. Studies show that the overconsumption of highly processed soy products can contribute to cancer and thyroid problems. Consume these products no more than two to four times per week.

Beans- Beans are one of the best sources of protein. There are numerous kinds and they are

so versatile, they can be eaten almost every day. Some people have gas troubles when they eat beans because their system is not used to them. Starting with easy to digest beans, such as lentils and split peas, can allow your body to slowly adjust. Then in a few weeks add others like, chickpeas, butter beans, and pigeon peas. Red beans and black beans are two of the hardest beans to digest; add those into your diet last. Soaking beans in water overnight, skimming the bubbles of foam off the top of them while they are cooking, as well as cooking them with kombu (kelp) helps to get rid of some of the gas. Keep canned and frozen beans on hand for a quick meal.

Nuts and Seeds- nuts and seeds are high in fat and protein. They can be eaten as snacks, in smoothies, on salads and as a garnish. Some people shy away from nuts because they are high in fat, but they are high in the fats that our body needs. Raw and freshly shelled nuts are best because as soon as they are shelled or heated, they begin to lose their nutrient content.

Almonds
Peanuts
Sesame seeds (gomazio)
Sunflower seeds
Pumpkin seeds
Walnuts
Pecans
Flax seeds (meal)
Hemp seeds

Tips on Using Seeds:
Flax, hemp and pumpkin seeds can be ground in a spice grinder then sprinkled over rice, cereal, salad, cous cous and more.

Seitan (say-tan or see-ten) also known as gluten (glue-ten), is made out of the protein in flour that holds bread together. It is made by a process of kneading and washing dough to remove as much starch as possible. The result is a chewy, meaty main dish that is high protein and can be sautéed, baked or fried. See page 99.

Other protein sources- there are other high protein foods such as quinoa and chlorella, please check page 39 for their protein amounts.

Fats and Oils

Fat is a nutrient we need for energy and to metabolize fat-soluble vitamins (Vitamins A, E, D & K). Oils are liquid fat. We need a mix of essential fatty acids, monounsaturated, polyunsaturated, and saturated fat everyday to keep our hair, skin and nails healthy, as well as to keep our joints, nerves

✳ VSG: VEGAN SOURCES OF FAT

Food	Amount	Mono	Poly	Sat	Omega 3	Omega 6
Avocado	1	19.6 g	3.6 g	4.2 g	.26	4.43 g
Peanut butter	2 tbsp	7.5 g	4.43 g	3.2 g	.196 g	35.5 g
Coconut (shredded)	¼ cup	1.6 g	.4 g	32 g	---	.396 g
Almonds	1 cup	45.9 g	17.4 g	5.5 g	.28 g	3.72 g
Walnuts	¼ cup	21 g	110.4 g	14.4 g	21.24 g	89.1 g
Pumpkin Seeds	¼ cup	4.9 g	7.2 g	2.9 g	.062 g	7.14 g
Flax seed (ground)	1 tbsp	.5 g	2.0 g	.3 g	1.59 g	.414 g
Pistachios	½ cup	14.3 g	8.2 g	3.3 g	.156 g	8.11 g
Olives	¼ cup	2.5 g	.26 g	1.2 g	.025 g	.340 g
Palm Oil	½ cup	39.9 g	10 g	53.24 g	.216 g	9.82 g
Peanut Oil	¼ cup	24.9 g	17.2 g	9.1 g	---	17.2 g
Sesame Oil	¼ cup	21.6 g	22.7 g	7.7 g	45 g	.163 g
Olive Oil	¼ cup	39.3 g	5.6 g	7.2 g	.4 g	4.4 g
Coconut Oil	¼ cup	3.15g	.97 g	47.1 g	---	.98 g
Hemp Oil	1 tbsp	---	10.5 g	1.5 g	2.5 g	8.0 g

and body lubricated and running smoothly. Most of the foods that contain fat have a mix of all type the different types of fat (mono, poly, and saturated). Then each food is classified depending on the amount of each type it contains. For vegans, fats are found in nuts, avocados, seeds, olives and oils.

Monounsaturated Fat- lowers harmful cholesterol and helps to prevent heart disease and cancer. Monounsaturated oils are liquid at room temperature and solid when refrigerated. Some sources of monounsaturated fats are: olives, olive oil and avocadoes.

Polyunsaturated Fat- can lower overall cholesterol, but too much can also reduce good cholesterol. Polyunsaturated oils are liquid at room temperature and when refrigerated. Some sources of polyunsaturated fats are: sunflower and flax seeds.

Saturated Fat- Saturated fat has gotten a bad rap over the years, but it is actually necessary to help assimilate fat soluble vitamins and build and maintain cells and

> Based on a 2,000 calorie a day diet, the recommended amount of fat needed is: 40-65 grams a day of total fat (mono, poly and saturated) with 20 of those grams from saturated fat.

hormones. Saturated fats are solid at room temperature. Some sources of saturated fats are: coconuts and palm oil.

EFA's- Essential Fatty Acids are a type of polyunsaturated oil and can only be obtained from food. EFA's come in two families, Omega-3 and Omega-6, and your body needs a balance of both to reduce cholesterol, support the thyroid and adrenal glands and promote healthy nerves, blood, arteries, skin and hair. Some sources of EFA's are: spirulina, flax and hemp seeds.

So what's all the fuss about?

Many of the oils (liquid fat) that we cook with as well as an overconsumption of fat can contribute to tumors, obesity, cancer and heart disease. In 2007, the big news was the health effects of trans-fats. In the 90's it was saturated fats, and I'm sure in 2027 it will be something else. Before the industrial revolution, butter, lard or vegetable oils were extracted by boiling or by a mortar and pestle type instrument. Highly processed and refined vegetable oils gained popularity based on a study of cholesterol claiming that saturated animal fats raised cholesterol, and ultimately raised the risk of heart disease. But, most vegetable oils found in grocery stores have been refined in some way. In the refining process, the oil is either solvent expressed or heated to high temperatures. When it's solvent expressed, toxic chemicals like hexane are added to them to extract the oil from the seed. After the oil has been extracted, it is heated to high temperatures (about 450°), bleached and deodorized to give them little or no taste.

When mono and poly unsaturated oils are heated above their smoking points (about 300°), free radicals can develop. An overabundance of free radicals in the body can lead to heart disease, premature aging and many forms of cancer.

According to the EPA (Environmental Protection Agency):

> Exposure of humans to high levels of hexane causes mild central nervous system (CNS) effects, including dizziness, giddiness, slight nausea, and headache. Chronic (long-term) exposure to hexane in air is associated with polyneuropathy(nerve disorder) in humans, with numbness in the extremities, muscular weakness, blurred vision, headache, and fatigue observed.

As of 2005, the EPA still had not fully studied the long-term health effects of hexane in humans, but is still allowing it to be used in our food.

HOW OILS ARE PROCESSED

Unrefined oil – The seed or the grain is pressed under low heat (no more than 160°-250°). Sometimes they are filtered once to remove residue. They retain vitamin E to help preserve and reduce rancidity (spoilage) which, in turn, reduces free radicals.

Refined oils- The seeds or the grains are heated at high temps up to 450°. They are chemically or expeller pressed, deodorized and depleted of lecithin, chlorophyll, vitamin E, beta-carotene, calcium, magnesium, iron, copper and phosphorus. Because refined oils are heated at high temperatures their free radical content increases.

Trans Fats

Trans Fats are a type of fat that occurs naturally in ruminant animals (cows, sheep) but the majority of trans-fats consumed today are from hydrogenated oils (see below). Consuming trans-fats can lead to obesity, heart disease, as well as colon, breast and prostate cancers. Trans fats are usually found in boxed, canned, frozen or fast food disguised under the name of hydrogenated or partially hydrogenated oils.

Hydrogenated Oils

Hydrogenated oils, also known as trans-fats, are polyunsaturated oils that are originally in a liquid state, but hydrogen is pumped into it to make it solid, kind of like butter. Hydrogenated oils are made to make polyunsaturated oils more stable, to give foods a buttery taste, to make things crispy like crackers and as a preservative to keep food sitting on the shelf longer. They are usually found in boxed, canned, fast food and margarine (including some soy margarines). These oils can cause heart disease, cancer, weight gain and blockage of necessary nutrients to be used in the body to help fight off disease.

A word about Canola Oil...

There is a lot of controversy about canola oil. It was originally made from the rapeseed. Because rapeseed is high in uric acid (can cause cancer, gout, mad cow disease and other health problems), a genetically modified version of the oil was made, Canola Oil (Canadian-Oil-low-acid), which is supposed to have less uric acid in it. But the process that canola oil goes through, high heating, deodorization and filtering causes the oil to accumulate free radicals. Scientists are now working on another genetically modified version to reverse this process. Hmmm... maybe avoiding it would be best.

What oil should I be using?

So all this talk about processing, refining and hydrogenation, I'm sure you are saying, "just tell me what to use," right? Cooking with oils that have been used for centuries in cultures that have little or no evidence of the heart disease and cancer that we have in our society seems to make sense. Freshly pressed oil is optimal but not realistic, so second best is buying unrefined, expeller-pressed organic oils. Here are some of the healthier oils to use:

Olive Oil is a monounsaturated oil that should be kept in a dark container to retain nutrients and keep from going rancid (bad). Extra virgin olive oil has the most nutrients and should be used on very low heat cooking, or not cooked at all.

Sesame Oil has been used for more than 4,000 years in Asia and can be used for medium/high heat cooking.

Palm Oil has been used in Africa for centuries for deep-frying and high heat frying. It received a bad rap in the U.S. when the fad of "no saturated fats" was going on. But now saturated fats, like palm and coconut, are becoming popular again. Red palm oil is high in beta-carotene and reduces blood cholesterol. White palm oil is made by boiling the red palm oil and is rich in antioxidants. White palm oil was used in the recipes in this book.

Peanut Oil is a monounsaturated fat that has been used in Africa and Asia for centuries. It can be used in medium/ high heat cooking. Peanuts are a common food allergen and should not be given to anyone with a food allergy.

Coconut Oil is a saturated fat that has been shown to help strengthen immunity and increase energy. It can be used for high heat cooking, pan frying and baking. It also has a light buttery flavor and has become one of the main oils I use.
Coconut oil has a very strong flavor so please use in small amounts or along with coconut milk until you get used to the flavor.

Flax seed Oil and **Hemp Oil** are very high in healthy Omega-3 and Omega-6 fats. These oils are very unstable when extracted from the seed, so it should come in a dark bottle and be kept in the refrigerator. These oils should never be heated or used in cooking.

NATURAL SWEETENERS

Carbohydrates such as fruit and brown rice contain whole natural sugars as a part of their structure. These sugars are utilized as energy in your body. Natural sweeteners such as honey, agave and maple syrup occur in nature and have gone through minimal or no processing. Most natural sweeteners retain the majority of their nutrients. Some can be used in healing processes, and if used in moderation, have a minimal effect on the body. Refined white and brown sugars can contribute to diabetes and osteoporosis by robbing the body and bones of essential vitamins and nutrients such as calcium and water.

Natural sweeteners

Diabetes
Nationally, 20.8 million people have diabetes and the number of children with it is rising every year. Diabetes is your body not being able to naturally regulate the amount of sugar (glucose) in your blood. More than 65 percent of people with diabetes die from stroke and heart attack. According to Tom Monte in the book, "The Complete Guide to Natural Healing,"

Dietary fat and cholesterol infiltrate the blood and block insulin from making glucose available for the cell.

In other words, a diet high in trans-fats, poor oils and cholesterol can make your blood so thick with plaque and fat, that it stops your organs from working properly. Also, just as sugar puts plaque on your teeth, it also puts plaque on your arteries. Even if you are not a vegan, improving your food choices will improve your health. And please, do not allow nutritional facts confuse you. Just because something has zero sugars does not mean it's healthy. Some artificial sweeteners are invented to have no sugar but your body still accepts it as that.

Agave nectar is syrup from a cactus type plant. It tastes like a mix of honey and maple syrup and can be used as a replacement for both. It has a very low glycemic index (dose not raise blood sugar), so that makes it wonderful for diabetics. Agave has trace amounts of calcium, magnesium, and potassium. Raw agave is best because it has gone through less processing and retains more of its nutrients than the non-raw variety.

Maple syrup is made by heating the sap from maple trees. It is high in potassium, calcium and B vitamins. Make sure to use 100% maple syrup to avoid artificial ingredients and high fructose corn syrup.

Honey is not considered vegan in all circles because it is made from bees. But it is a natural sweetener and usually less expensive than agave or maple syrup. Many vegans still use honey because of its healing properties and it is high in amino acids, calcium, potassium, and phosphorus. It can be substituted for agave or maple syrup in these recipes.
Note: Do not give honey to children under the age of two years because their digestive systems are not mature enough to digest a bacteria present in honey which could cause a serious illness called botulism.

Brown Rice Syrup is made from rice and has a mild light taste. It's not as sweet as other sweeteners so it's great for diabetics.

Black Strap Molasses- molasses is the syrup resulting from the processing of sugar. It's basically made of all of the nutrients that have been removed from white sugar. It's very high in iron and calcium. Because of its strong flavor, can be used along with maple syrup and agave and should not be used alone unless you are used to it.

Stevia is an herb that has a naturally sweet flavor. It regulates blood sugar, soothes the intestines and stomach and helps prevent decay. It comes in powdered, liquid or herbal forms. It tastes similar to Equal™.

Sucanat is made by boiling all of the water out of sugar cane. It is less processed than evaporated cane juice and turbinado (raw sugar) and it still contains trace amount of the vitamins and nutrients because it has not been stripped of its color. Sucanat costs the least among the more nutritious natural sweeteners and is great for baking. Sucanat has minimal amounts of potassium, vitamin A, calcium, magnesium and other minerals. I've been seeing a "white" version of sucanat in stores lately but the darker it is, the better.

How much sugar are we *really* eating?
The World Health Organization (WHO) recommends that less than 10 percent of our total calorie intake should be from refined sugar. Some say that you should not have any at all.

The Recommended Daily allowances are:
Children- 25g (5.26 teaspoons) on a 1000-calorie diet,

Women/teens 40 g (8.43 teaspoons) on a 1,600-calorie diet,

Active men and women 48 grams (10.1 teaspoons) on a 2,200-calorie diet

These allowances are recommended, but ten teaspoons of refined sugar a day is too much for anybody. This is one reason diabetes and obesity are as prevalent as they are today. But how much are we really consuming?

Food	Amount	Sugar (g)	Sugar (tsp)
Post Raisin Bran	1 cup	15.71	3.31
Cola	21 oz	43.59	9.18
Snickers	1 bar	30	6.32
Chips Ahoy Cookies	3	39	8.21
Ben & Jerry's Ice Cream Chunky Monkey	½ cup	28	5.9
Sunny Delight	16 oz	58	12.2
Gatorade	16 oz	28	5.9
Whole Milk	1 cup	12.83	6
Yogurt (plain skim)	1 cup	18.82	9

Beware of the Boot Leg Natural Sweeteners!

I have started to see the words evaporated cane juice, dried cane juice, crystallized cane juice, milled cane sugar and organic sugar on many items in the health food store. For a while I bought into purchasing them assuming that they were somehow better for me than white sugar. Then one day I actually saw evaporated cane juice for sale on the shelf and it looked almost exactly like white sugar. These sugars are passed off as natural sugars but are almost as processed as white sugar. The majority of vitamins and minerals have been removed meaning they will have the same effect on your body as white sugar. Don't fall for the fake one's:

*Evaporated cane juice

*Brown sugar with caramel coloring

*Organic sugar

*Turbinado

*Sugar in the raw

WATER, MILKS AND BEVERAGES

Water is one of the most essential nutrients and you can only live about four days without it. Adults need eight to twelve 8-ounce glasses a day, and children should drink at least half their

**Be on
the lookout:**
Decaffeinated tea is usually black tea with the caffeine removed from it using harmful chemicals.

body weight in ounces for hydration. Drinking other liquids cannot substitute for water. Caffeine and sugar laced drinks can dehydrate the body so are not a substitute. A few symptoms of dehydration are headaches, vomiting, fatigue, dry mouth, arthritis, constipation and joint pain.

Herbal Tea has been used for thousands of years and comes in forms such as, green, black and white. Tea can be used for healing like drinking red raspberry leaf for PMS cramps, or just for enjoyment such as peppermint tea in the morning. Usually as a rule, most black tea (leaf) has caffeine. Green tea has very small amounts of caffeine where its healing properties outweigh its caffeine levels. Herbal tea's (ex: chamomile, peppermint) are naturally caffeine free.

Milks

There are so many different types of non-dairy milks out today. Soy, rice, almond, hemp, coconut, oat and kefir are the most common. People who are allergic to nuts or soy may want to stick with rice, hemp, coconut or oat milk. If you do use soymilk please buy organic. I have also recently noticed that many alternative milk companies are starting to use evaporated cane juice and all I know is it's becoming harder and harder to find foods without added refined sweetener's. Fortunately some brands have started to make the unsweetened variety but they can be hard to find.

Juices and Smoothies

Freshly squeezed or juiced fruits and vegetables are the best kinds of juice. They are rich in enzymes and vitamins and help promote healing and detoxification. Bottled juices made from 100% juice is more nutritious than juice drinks with added sweeteners, but they should still be consumed in moderation because they are processed and have a high natural sugar content.

Smoothies are great snacks or meal replacers. They can be made using fruits, milks, spirulina and nut butters so that they are jam-packed full of nutrients. Pre made smoothies may have added artificial sweeteners and evaporated cane juice, so don't assume it's healthy just because it's a smoothie. Please read your labels.

SEA VEGGIES

Seaweeds or sea vegetables are a wonderful whole food supplement to add to your lifestyle. They are rich in vitamins, minerals, protein and essential fatty acids. They are healing, nourishing, cleansing and blood building. Sea vegetables help to protect against radiation, improve anemia, regulate blood sugar, strengthen your immune system, and reduce cysts and tumors. Even though these vegetables are high in B12 the few studies that have been done show that humans may not assimilate their form of the vitamin, so it cannot be counted on as a reliable source.

Sea Vegetables

Kombu (com-boo), also known as **Kelp**, is high in minerals, especially B vitamins. It is a rich source of iodine, helpful in treating thyroid problems. Kelp helps to decrease gas in beans, increase the digestibility of food, reduce tumors, soothe the lungs and throat and boost the nutritional value of the food it's cooked in. Use it like a bay leaf while cooking, cut it into pieces, or use the granules to add to soups, sauces, salads or as a garnish.

Spirulina is a blue/green algae that is traditional to African and Mexican people. Spirulina is high in protein and improves energy. It helps heal the liver and kidneys from damage caused by alcohol, prescription medication and overconsumption of animal foods. Because it's high in chlorophyll, EFA's, iron, beta-carotene and other nutrients, it is helpful to people suffering from, cancer, diabetes and arthritis. Spirulina comes in tablets or powdered form and can be used in smoothies, cookies, and ice cream.

Chlorella is an algae that has one of the highest concentrations of chlorophyll of any food. Chlorophyll is what makes plants green and is high in iron, and helps prevent cancer. Chlorella is a great source of protein and helps speed the cleansing of blood. Due to chlorella's high nutritional content, it's useful in all immune diseases, normalizes blood pressure and blood sugar, and helps to safely remove PCB's (pollutant), pesticides and heavy metals from your body. It can be taken in a tablet or powdered form. If taken in the powdered form, add it to juices and smoothies. Chlorella is more expensive than most seaweed, but a little goes a long way.

Nori is that greenish blackish looking "skin" or wrap on a sushi roll. It usually comes in flakes or sheets. Nori is high in calcium and vitamins B and C, and it aids in digesting fried foods.

Sea moss- Also known as Irish moss or carageenan, sea moss usually comes either ground up or whole as a soft yellowish branch. Sea moss relieves congestion, helps treat ulcers, and soothes the respiratory and digestive systems. It can be added to smoothies as a nutrient boost and to soothe dry lungs. In the Caribbean, sea moss is used to make a sweet milky drink. As carrageenan, it is used as a thickener in soups and dairy products. I prefer the whole plant to the ground up moss, but either will work. Look in Asian or Caribbean grocery stores to find the whole plant and at health food stores for the ground up version.

Making Sea Moss

1. Soak 1 pack of sea moss overnight in enough water to cover it. (If using ground skip step 1)

2. Remove from the refrigerator; pick out black or dark sections, strain and rinse. If using powdered, rinse 1 ½ cup in a small strainer.

3. Add 8 cups of water to a medium/large pot and bring to a boil.

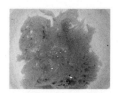

4. Add sea moss and reduce the heat to med/low.

5. Simmer on low until it's completely dissolved, stirring occasionally (about 20 min). Stir more in the last 5-8 minutes to help dissolve.

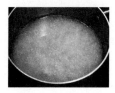

6. Turn moss off and add 2 tbsp of flax seed meal and mix well.

7. Let sea moss cool for about 30 min then pour into 2 ice trays. You can also keep some in the fridge if you plan to use it in the next 3-4 days.

8. Once frozen, the cubes can be taken out as needed and used in smoothies or drinks.

FERMENTED FOODS

Fermented foods contain microorganisms that are similar to the beneficial microorganisms or bacteria found in the human intestinal tract. They are also called "friendly bacteria" or "probiotics". They are useful for a healthy digestive tract and immune system and have been used for thousands of years. Probiotics are available to consumers mainly in the form of dietary supplements and foods.

 The World Health Organization and the Food and Agriculture Organization of the United Nations, defines probiotics as "live microorganisms, which, when administered in adequate amounts, confer a health benefit on the host." In probiotic foods and supplements, the bacteria may have been present originally or added during preparation. Lactobacillus and Bifidobacteria are common types of bacteria found in fermented foods. There is a lot of legal and scientific research and "naming" of the type of organisms and foods that can be labeled a probiotic. Soon there will be only certain foods and products that can be labeled this way due to the genus, species and strain of the exact bacteria in the product. This type of labeling is being done so that probiotics can be used and promoted as a treatment for diseases and health conditions.

 Foods containing probiotics: yogurt, fermented milk, kefir, miso, tempeh, sauerkraut, kimchi, injera, amazake, kombucha, sour dough, apple cider vinegar as well as some juices and soy beverages.

HERBS, SPICES, AND CONDIMENTS

When some people think of vegetarian food, they think of bland carrots and lettuce. Fortunately that does not have to be so. Herbs, spices and condiments have been used for thousands of years and can not only enhance the flavor of food but can also be beneficial for your health.

Herbs and Spices

Here are a few spices and seasonings that are commonly used in soulfood, along with some of their health benefits:

Red pepper flakes are high in vitamins A, C, E, and selenium and strengthens the immune system.

Garlic (powder) treats hypertension, infections, high blood pressure, reduces cholesterol and fat in the arteries, fights colds, yeast infections, bacteria and worms.

Onion (powder) contains B vitamins and is useful in expelling mucous.

Chili powder is high in vitamins A, B1 and C.

Paprika helps relieve sinus troubles and colds. It's high in Vitamins A, C, B2, & B3.

Thyme helps relieve headaches, colds, hypothyroidism, worms, loss of appetite and diarrhea.

Cayenne pepper is high in Vitamins A, B and C.

Parsley is a rich source of antioxidants, folic acid, iron and vitamins A, C and K. Not recommended in large amounts for pregnant women.

Condiments

Condiments are prepared foods that can add wonderful flavors to your meals. Some may be more processed than others and should be used minimally. Condiments such as mustard, ketchup, mayonnaise (vegan), bar-b-que sauce and salsa can all be found organically made. I've mentioned a few condiments below that may be unfamiliar.

Nutritional Yeast

Nutritional Yeast is a fungus that is present naturally on fruits and vegetables. The earliest recorded use was in 1559 BC, Egypt. Now nutritional yeast is made from growing the yeast on molasses, which makes it high in B vitamins and is one of the few sources of Vitamin B12 for vegans. It is also a complete protein and regulates blood sugar levels for people with low blood sugar. It has a slightly nutty/cheesy flavor and is used in sauces, gravies, popcorn topping and as a cheese substitute. Nutritional yeast comes in a powder or flake form, but avoid the canned version because it does not taste good. Try the Red Star brand or the kind in bulk bins.

Soy Sauce is made from fermented soybeans, wheat and salt and is commonly used in Asian cuisines. It can be used as a meat-flavoring substitute in vegan cooking. Try to find the brands that do not contain caramel coloring. For those with allergies or high blood pressure, wheat free and low sodium brands are available.

Bragg's liquid amino acids is made with soybeans and is similar to soy sauce but with a lighter flavor. Braggs can be used on tofu, in gravies and sauces, dressings, soups and sautéed veggies. Bragg's can usually be found in health food stores, but can sometimes be found in grocery stores as well.

READING LABELS

Additives and Preservatives

Using additives and preservatives is a natural process that has been practiced for thousands of years partly for survival, food variety and to fully utilize the entire yearly crop. Natural preserving can be done using vinegar, citric acid (lemons), salt, drying, as well as heating and canning. These methods keep food edible for up to a year, which is really long enough. Nowadays, the processed food industry uses additives and preservatives that are artificial chemicals. These chemicals are

INGREDIENTS: WHEAT GLUTEN, WATER, EN-RICHED WHEAT FLOUR (WHEAT FLOUR, NIACIN, IRON, THIAMIN MONONITRATE, RIBOFLAVIN, FOLIC ACID), YELLOW CORN MEAL, SUGAR, SOYBEAN OIL, CORN STARCH. CONTAINS 2% OR LESS OF CORN SYRUP SOLIDS, SALT, DEX-TROSE, CULTURED WHEY, EGG WHITE SOLIDS, LEAVENING (SODIUM ACID PYROPHOSPHATE, SODIUM BICARBONATE, MONOCALCIUM PHOSPHATE), CARRAGEENAN, HYDROLYZED CORN, SOY, AND WHEAT PROTEIN, BROWN SUGAR, NATURAL FLAVORS FROM NON-MEAT SOURCES, TORULA YEAST, SPICES, SOY PRO-TEIN ISOLATE, IODIZED SALT, ONION POWDER, GARLIC POWDER, NATURAL SMOKE FLAVOR, HYDROLYZED TORULA AND BREWER'S YEAST PROTEIN, CELLULOSE GUM, SOY FIBER, AU-TOLYZED YEAST EXTRACT, PAPRIKA FOR COLOR, XANTHAN GUM, DISODIUM GUANYL-ATE, DISODIUM INOSINATE, POTASSIUM CHLORIDE, RED #3 AND BLUE #1 FOR COLOR.

CONTAINS SOY, WHEAT, MILK AND EGG INGREDIENTS.

used for color enhancement, taste improvement, and so that they can have a long shelf life, meaning they can be in the grocery store longer. One thing these companies don't tell you is that the additives and preservatives they add to the food can cause serious health problems. The FDA and USDA, along with these companies, mislead us by saying food is "all natural" or "no sugar added" to confuse us into thinking we are making wise food choices, even though the foods may contain high fructose corn syrup, aspartame or whatever new chemical is in at the moment.

Attempting to decipher the ingredients list on food packages can be a very challenging thing. There are thick books that break down each chemical that is now added to our food.

Being and becoming a healthy vegan means that you have to read labels and educate yourself on what foods may have animal products or harmful ingredients. If you read anything that you are not familiar with you probably should not buy it. The following list describes some of the most common and harmful additives and preservatives to watch out for.

Top 11 Additives and Preservatives to avoid

1. **High Fructose Corn Syrup (HFCS)** is a processed, refined sweetener made from corn. Studies show that HFCS can lead to fatty liver, obesity, heart disease, cramps, bloating, and loose stools. It can be found in desserts, sodas, candy, processed foods (crackers, cake, bread) jelly, fruit and fruit drinks.

2. **Monosodium Glutamate (MSG)** also known as glutamic acid is a preservative that is used to enhance the flavor of food. It can be naturally found in certain seaweeds,

✷ VSG: BUYER BEWARE!

If a package has changed, the ingredients have probably also changed.

I have a favorite type of non-dairy ice cream and I enjoy this brand because it has a great flavor and pretty natural ingredients. It used to be sold only in health food stores but now I see it in most major chain grocery stores and even Wal-Mart. But one day when I was about to buy some of their ice cream sandwiches I noticed the box had changed. Come to find out, they had added HIGH FRUCTOSE CORN SYRUP!!! I was so upset I actually emailed the company (something I had never done before) and expressed my disappointment. They wrote me back and thanked me and pointed me to their other products, which did not have it. This taught me to constantly read labels even if it's a brand I've bought for years. As small companies grow, they sometimes get bought out by larger companies (like Odwalla who is now owned by Coke) and the quality of their product changes. Or as businesses grow they have to compete with the demand while still making a profit so they may add in an artificial flavor here or there to replace real ingredients.

but a refined version of it is used in many processed foods. MSG can also come under the name: hydrolyzed protein, textured protein, autolyzed protein, yeast extract, autolyzed yeast extract, protein isolate, modified food starch, modified corn starch, calcium caseinate, sodium caseinate and sometimes natural flavor. Studies show that MSG can cause cancer, migraine headaches, allergies, chest pains, asthma attacks, diarrhea, depression and mood swings. MSG can be found in processed and packaged foods, seasoned salt, Chinese food, processed meat, broths and bullion cubes.

Speaking of Chinese Food...
Chinese restaurants can be found in almost every city in America. They are vegan friendly and usually very affordable. Unfortunately many Chinese restaurants use MSG in their food. If a restaurant does not promote that they don't use MSG, they probably do. Please ask for NO MSG.

3. **Hydrogenated/Partially Hydrogenated Oils-** Also known as trans-fats, hydrogenated or partially hydrogenated oils are oils that naturally come in a liquid form that are pumped with hydrogen to make them into a solid form, like margarine. This product is cheaper to use and produce. Hydrogenated oils can lead to heart disease, increased cholesterol, hardened arteries, clogged arteries, and cause or contribute to cancer. They can be found in chips, crackers, cookies, bread and margarine.

4. **Hidden cow's milk and dairy-** Milk in food can come under names like: casein, whey, sodium caseinate, lactose and sodium lactylate. These forms of milk can manifest in the body as hives, rashes, breathing difficulty, eczema, mucus, stomach and intestinal pain. These ingredients and additives can be found in sauces, gravies, soy/rice cheeses, drinks, protein powders, candy bars, flavored potato chips and more.

5. **Food Coloring** is used to enhance the color of processed foods, as well as to appeal to children. They are found in sodas, candy, ice cream, bread, meat, cereal, baked goods, canned fruits, juices and drinks. Food coloring comes under many names, but here are two of the most harmful.
   Red #40 may cause a skin rash, nausea and hyperactivity in young children.
   Yellow #5 may cause allergies, asthma, migraine headache, anxiety, clinical depression, hyperactivity in children. It is also a possible carcinogen (causes cancer).

6. **Natural Flavors-** Many "natural flavorings" are used to enhance the taste of food because it has been processed so much that the original flavor has been lost. Hundreds of different chemicals are used under the term "natural flavorings," including MSG. An example is:

   Buttery flavor (diacetyl) may lead to lung disease. It is found in microwave popcorn and crackers.

Sodium benzoate has been recently found to cause cancer, brain and nerve disorders and DNA alterations. It is found in soft drinks, pickles, sauces and juice drinks.

7. **BHA/BHT** is used to stop oils from going bad on the shelf. They may cause cancer, allergic reactions and may be toxic to the liver and nervous system. This preservative is found in butter, meats, cereals, chewing gum, baked goods, snack foods, dehydrated potatoes and beer.

8. **Aspartame** is an artificial sweetener used as a sugar substitute (Equal™, Nutri Sweet™). According to the Department of Health and Human Services, it can cause cancer, vision problems, seizures, brain and nerve damage, headaches, dizziness, mood swings, abdominal cramps, fatigue, behavioral problems, hyperactivity, and allergies. It can be found in diet soft drinks, tabletop sweeteners, pudding/Jell-O™, lemonade, Kool-Aid™, iced tea, gum, ice cream, cereal, "sugar free" and diet products.

9. **Sugar and Sweeteners-** Sugar comes under many different names such as: brown sugar, high fructose corn syrup, high maltose corn syrup, maltodextrin, sucrose, fructose and dextrose. Sugar can lead to obesity, cavities, diabetes and hypoglycemia, increased triglycerides (blood fats) or Candida (yeast). You can find it in everything from bread, gravy, candy and fruit drinks to french fries.

10. **Gelatin** is made from a by-product of the meat industry that is a mix of cow bones and hides, pigskins and fish bladders. It is used to make hair and body products, gel capsules for certain vitamins, in marshmallows, as a filler for some wines, and in Jell-O™ and other desserts.

11. **Caffeine** is a stimulant that weakens the body, causes high blood pressure, increases plaque build up in the arteries, inhibits fertility, and causes circulation problems by making blood vessels constrict. ✦

❊ VSG: FiNDiNG Balance

As a parent and for myself, I try to practice balance by using what works best for me and my family's bodies. Once I was at someone's house and 15 kids were walking around with popsicles and I didn't bring a snack for my son, and he looked at me with those big eyes and asked if he could have one. Was I going to say no when he asked me for some? I knew the popsicle probably had red #40 and high fructose corn syrup, but I let him have it. When we got home I had him drink some water and gave him some blood cleansing herbal tea to counteract what he just ate. When he was younger I used to say no, and I still rarely say yes to things like that. I've learned my balance, however, as he gets older, he must begin to find his own as well. Teaching your children wise food choices is empowering!

CHAPTER 5
DINING OUT
& MENU GUIDE

TYPES OF RESTAURANTS

ORDERING FROM RESTAURANT MENUS

TIPS ON FOODS TO AVOID

DINING OUT

Dining out can open up a whole new world. Trying different varieties and ethnicities of foods can add spice to your regular dining routine. The smells, décor, and spices of a new restaurant can be an experience in itself. Sometimes when you try new cuisines your palette (range of foods you enjoy) has to get used to it. I know the first time I tried Thai food, I had some soup that had a super strong ginger flavor. I had never tasted ginger before and the flavor was so vibrant that I sent it back and had the nerve to say I did not like it. But now I

love ginger and use it all the time in cooking and for its healing properties as well. So if you try a new restaurant, be opened minded. Tell your server your general likings and ask for suggestions and clarity where you are unfamiliar. Please keep in mind that there are some restaurants that are better than others so be open to trying different restaurants of the same cuisine until you find one you like. Also, don't be afraid to talk to other customers and ask them what they ordered if it looks good to you. Ask them if they have been there before and what their favorite thing is. You can also ask your waiter what is her/his favorite dish. Eating out is fun and can be used as a substitute for having to cook yourself, but too much eating out is not the best for your health. Many restaurants use a lot of added salt and sugar, only serve white rice or pasta and cook with poor and overly used oils. Too much of this food in excess can cause health problems. Balance is key, and if you have to eat out a lot, try to choose restaurants that buy fresh ingredients and make their food from scratch daily. Also, check your phone book or the Internet for different restaurants in your area. Call and politely inform them that you are a vegetarian, ask them about their menu and ask if foods can be made with no butter, milk, yogurt, eggs, or meat broths. While you are eating out, if your order happens to come out with cheese milk or butter, no need to get upset, people do things out of habit. Just send it back. Enjoy!

Restaurants

Since looking at new menus can become overwhelming and you may not know what to order, here is a list of restaurant cuisines that are usually vegan friendly, no matter where you are in the world, as well as a list of suggested items to order. Most restaurants serve white rice and pasta but sometimes they have brown rice if you ask. Also, unfortunately most restaurants don't have any vegan desserts unless you are at a vegan restaurant. Sometimes you can find a sorbet (frozen fruit style ice cream with no dairy).

THAI/ MALAYSIAN: Thai food is one of my favorite cuisines! It is a form of Asian food that is similar to Chinese but uses more pungent and distinct spices. Be sure to ask for everything with no egg.

Suggested foods: Masuman or Penang curry dishes, Roti Canai with no chicken, Basil rice, Coconut rice, Brown rice, Pineapple fried rice, Pad Thai, sautéed vegetables with fried tofu, Basil Tofu, Pad See U (noodles with tasty brown sauce), Tom Kha (delicious coconut soup), Miso soup, Edammame, Vegetable dumplings and Vegetable spring rolls.

MEXICAN: Mexican restaurants are very popular and can be found just about anywhere. Ask for foods with no cheese, lard or sour cream.

Suggested foods: Vegetable fajitas, vegetable enchiladas, tacos, plantains, burrito with rice, beans, lettuce, and tomato, Pico de Gallo sauce, guacamole, corn tortillas, salsa, taco salad with rice, beans and veggies.

An Ethiopian meal

ETHIOPIAN: is an ancient African Cuisine that you eat with your hands using a spongy bread called injera. This is my all time family favorite.
Suggested foods: The veggie combo, that consists of greens, split peas, lentils, green beans, cabbage, potatoes and carrots, Samboosas (fried vegetable pocket), Timatim salad and Tej (honey wine).

CARIBBEAN: Food from the Caribbean Islands use a lot of curries and hot spices.

Suggested meals: Jerk, curry, or bbq tofu with vegetables, plantains, rice and peas, veggie patty, veggie roti (vegetables and chick peas in a large wrap), sea moss drink, mango juice, ginger beer (watch for sugar sweeteners and ask if they have honey instead).

CHINESE: Chinese food can be found in almost every city and small town across America. Just make sure to ask them not to add any egg or MSG.

Suggested meals: Fried tofu with mixed vegetables, vegetable spring roll, vegetable fried rice, Chinese broccoli, brown rice, vegetable noodle soup, broccoli in garlic sauce, kung pau tofu, chow fun, steamed of fried vegetable dumplings, sesame tofu/veggie chicken, General Tso's tofu/ veggie chicken, and vegetable lo-mein.

An Indian meal

INDIAN: Indian food has wonderful flavors and many of the foods come in delicious sauces. Ask for food with no yogurt or ghee, which are dairy products.

Suggested meals: Okra, spinach and potatoes, rice, chana masala) curried chickpeas with veggies, Dahl (lentils), aloo gobi (potatoes and cauliflower) parata (bread), nan (bread), samosa, pakora (vegetable fritters), masala dosa (bread filled with potato and vegetable), cauliflower and chana (chickpeas), tamarind sauce and mango chutney.

AMERICAN: it can be difficult to find a satisfying meal at an American deli or café style restaurant, but sometimes that may be your only choice. Ask for no sour cream, butter, milk or cheese.
Suggested meals: Vegetable or bean soup, salad with Italian dressing, steamed vegetable of the day, rice and beans, dry toast with peanut butter and jelly, baked potato with vegetables and olive oil, fruit salad or fruit juice.

Vegetarian (American)- Many of these restaurants are not necessarily vegan. They may use butter, eggs, milk, yogurt and cheese. Ask for you meal made without any of these.
Suggested meals: Noodles, rice, beans, veggies, veggie burgers, soup, salad, tofu, and vegan desserts.

Soulfood: Many soulfood restaurants have started to sell vegetables with no meat. Some may use butter in their vegetables or chicken stock in their rice. Be sure to ask about this. Also be on the lookout for the use of sugar.
Suggested Meals: Vegetable plate, bread, salad, collard greens, green beans, rice, yams, potatoes, black eyed peas and lima beans.

ITALIAN: Italian can be very satisfying, especially if you love pasta. Be sure to emphasize no cheese or butter. Some restaurants now have whole-wheat pasta as an option, but most do not, so eat this in moderation.
Suggested meals: Salad with olive oil and lemon, broccoli rabe', steamed or sautéed veggie of the day, pasta with marinara sauce and vegetables, bruchetta, pizza with vegetables and no cheese.

MEDITERRANEAN: Mediterranean food is a very light cuisine, using a lot of fresh ingredients and whole foods.
Suggested meals: Hummus (chickpea dip) with pita, tabouleh (salad made form bulgur wheat, stuffed grape leaves, baba ganoush (eggplant dip), falafel (fried chickpea patty), lentil soup, fried cauliflower, chickpeas, salad and baklava (phyllo dough dessert with nuts and honey).

JAPANESE: Very popular now so it's easy to find. It is very light and healthy. Many times you can find "sushi" style nori rice rolls in grocery stores.
Suggested meals: Vegetable tempura roll, avocado, cucumber and carrot roll, edammame, miso soup, tofu with mixed vegetables and seaweed salad.

THE MALL: The mall is a place where you might find yourself during your lunch break or with your family on the weekend. Surprisingly there are a few vegan options. Try to stay away from fast food chains like Taco Bell and stick to places that may cook their food fresh daily.

Suggested Meals: Chinese food, pasta with marinara sauce, bean burritos, vegetable plates at soulfood restaurants, smoothies made with juice and no yogurt or milk and french fries.

Traveling

Hotel Dining: Please take advantage of complimentary breakfast and room service. Many times room service is more than willing to make you something with whatever ingredients they have on hand.

Suggested meals:

Breakfast- Dry toast with peanut butter and jelly. Oatmeal sweetened with honey or maple syrup, potatoes or hash browns, orange juice, fruit/ fruit salad, tea with honey.

Room service- pasta with marinara sauce, french fries, sandwich with sautéed veggies and mustard, garden salad with Italian dressing, pizza with no cheese topped with veggies and marinara sauce.

Road trips: If you are going on a road trip or on an airplane, it is easier to bring your own snacks and food. You can request a no dairy vegetarian meal on planes but they are not very tasty. If you are taking a long trip, bring a small cooler so you can keep your food longer. *Items to pack:* Sandwiches, wraps, nori rolls, fruit salad, trail mix, plain chips, corn chips and salsa, nuts, burritos, cookies, granola bars, pasta salad, hummus, bean dip, carrot chips and more.

Vending machines: Believe it or not there are actually some vegan choices in vending machines. Some of the items may contain sugar but if you ever find yourself stuck in a bus station or just need something quick here are some suggestions: peanuts, Nature Valley granola bars, plain potato chips, water and 100 percent juice.

FOODS TO REDUCE/AVOID

Processed foods- Processed food is any food that has been changed from its natural state or has been created in a laboratory or factory. Most things in a box, can, or package can be considered processed food. These foods include: white flour products, white rice, sugar, candy, cookies, bread and chips. Highly refined processed foods cause the body to gain weight, because they are void of necessary nutrients. They leach vitamins and minerals out of your body which in turn, keeps you craving for more until your nutritional needs are met. Processed foods can also weaken the body by causing chronic yeast infections, constipation, bloating and weight gain as well as stressing the pancreas to release large amounts of insulin, which can lead to diabetes and more.

Caffeine is a stimulant that weakens the body, causes high blood pressure, increases plaque build up in the arteries, inhibits fertility, and causes circulation problems by making blood vessels constrict.

How much caffeine are we consuming?

Studies suggest that consuming no more than 150 mg of caffeine daily (for adults) should be a safe amount to avoid the health effects. Some say we don't need any. How much are you consuming?

Food/item	Amount	Caffeine
Coffee	12 oz	142 mg
Espresso	2 oz	128 mg
Diet Cola (1 can)	1 can	57 mg
Regular hot tea	8 oz	47 mg
Red Bull energy drink	1 can	76 mg
Decaf coffee	12 oz	4 mg
Starbucks coffee	16 oz	223-320 mg

Soda and juice drinks

Soda and Juice Drinks are filled with sugars, high fructose corn syrup, artificial flavors and caffeine. This can contribute to hyperactivity in kids, diabetes, allergies, weight gain and obesity. Diet sodas also contain aspartame (see page 71).

Microwave Foods

Radiation can cause cancer and a mutation in your DNA (your genes) that can be passed on to your child. Research shows that radiation from microwaves can cause risks such as, reduction of the amount of nutrients in your food and mutation in the chemical make-up of your food. This process can lead to a build up of free radicals in your blood ultimately causing premature aging and cancer. The FDA and the USDA do not know the health effects of microwave radiation because they have not done any long-term studies on humans. In spite of this lack of knowledge, microwaves are allowed to be used everyday to heat our food.

Fast Food

One fast food meal can exceed your body's daily needs of salt, fat, cholesterol, and calories. This can contribute to high blood pressure, cancer, heart disease, diabetes and obesity. If you get a chance, watch the movie *Super Size Me* about the health effects of fast food. ✦

✳ VSG: 6 TIPS TO DO EVERYDAY TO HELP IMPROVE YOUR HEALTH

1. **Eat a green vegetable at every meal.** Green vegetables are high in Vitamins C, A, and K, calcium, iron and fiber. They help to maintain your weight, build a strong immune system and keep your colon clean.

2. **Eat raw fruits and vegetables everyday.** Live fruits and veggies contain enzymes, which help reduce aging and promote and facilitate many necessary body functions. These foods also will help you cleanse toxins out of the body and repair damage caused by eating fast food, microwaved food, pesticides and additives.

3. **Drink water or 100% juice instead of soda.** Drink 8-12 eight-ounce servings (64 to 96 oz) of water a day. Children should drink half their body weight in ounces. Juice should be kept at a minimum unless it is freshly made.

4. **Eat whole grains.** Whole grains help to maintain your energy through the day and curb your sweet cravings.

5. **Turn off the TV/Radio.** Commercials run all day, keeping our minds focused on super-sizing and overindulging. Use that time to read, write, exercise, or meditate.

6. **Exercise**- Exercise helps to keep your body fit and in shape. Being a vegan can help to keep your weight down, but working out keeps you toned and in shape. Also you may lose some weight when you become a vegan and lifting weights can help to build muscle and put on more weight.

Also, try to cook at least one to five meals per week containing: protein (beans, tofu, seitan), greens (collard, kale, or broccoli), a grain (brown rice) or a sweet vegetable (sweet potato, squash, or plantain). One balanced meal a week is better than none.

CHAPTER 6
RECIPES & MORE!

RECIPES

MENU PLANNING

TIPS ON FOODS TO AVOID

BREAKFAST

Fresh Fruit Kebobs

Ingredients:

10 wood skewers

Cantaloupe

Watermelon

Strawberries

Pineapple

Grapes

Peaches

Plums

Or your favorite fruit

Directions:

1. Cut the fruit in bite size pieces except for the grapes and strawberries. They can be kept whole or cut in half.
2. Alternately place the fruit on the kebob until full.

Party of 6-10

+ GLUTEN AND SOY FREE +

Hearty Breakfast Potatoes

Ingredients:

¼ cup oil

3 potatoes (about 3 cups), cubed

½ cup chopped onions

¼ cup green peppers

3 cloves of chopped garlic

1 tsp granulated garlic

1 tsp granulated onion

1 tsp sea salt

½ tsp black pepper

½ tsp dry basil

¼ cup of vegetable broth

1 tbsp fresh parsley

Directions:

1. Heat a cast iron or nonstick skillet on medium heat then add the oil.
2. Add the potatoes to the pan and lay flat. Cook on medium heat for 5 minutes.
3. After 5 minutes, one side should be brown. Turn potatoes over and add onions, green peppers and garlic.
4. Lay flat and cook for 5 more minutes turning and laying flat every 2-3 minutes.
5. Add spices (except parsley) and ¼ cup vegetable broth then cook for 5 minutes turning every 2-3 minutes.
6. Lay flat and let sit for 2 minutes on medium heat. Mix then lay flat again for 2 minutes. If needed Add 2 more tbsp of oil.
7. Top with parsley.

★ *Quick Tip: Use leftover baked potatoes and cut the cooking time in half.*

Party of 4

+ GLUTEN AND SOY FREE +

Satisfy My Soul Grits

Ingredients:

1 tsp oil

1cup corn

¼ cup onions

1 small jalapeño cut in ¼" rounds

1 cup grits

4 cups of water

½ tsp sea salt

¼ cup nutritional yeast

1 tbsp non-GMO vegan margarine or olive oil

Directions:

1. Using a medium pan, sauté corn, onions and jalapeños in oil for until soft. 5 minutes
2. Add the water and grits to the pot and bring to boil.
3. Reduce heat to low and simmer for 10 minutes stirring occasionally.
4. Add nutritional yeast and mix well. Simmer for a 2-3 more minutes.

Party of 4- 6

+ GLUTEN AND SOY FREE +

Sun-day Grits

Ingredients:

4 cups water

1 tsp sea salt

1 tbsp non GMO vegan margarine or olive oil

1 cup yellow corn grits

Directions:

1. Add all ingredients to a small pot and bring to a boil.
2. Reduce the heat to low. Cover and let simmer for 10 minutes, stirring occasionally.
3. If you like your grits more runny add ¼ of water at a time until your desired consistency.

Party of 4- 6

+ GLUTEN AND SOY FREE +

Stacks

Dry ingredients:
1¼ cups whole wheat or spelt flour

1 tbsp flax seed meal

2 tsp baking powder
(aluminum free)

¼ tsp salt

Wet ingredients:
2 tbsp oil

1 – 1½ cup of almond
(or non dairy) milk

2 tbsp pure maple syrup

½ tsp pure vanilla

Directions:
1. Mix dry ingredients together in a medium bowl.
2. Mix the wet ingredients in a small bowl.
3. Make a hole in the center of dry ingredients and pour the wet into it and mix. The batter should be a little lumpy.
4. Heat a cast iron or no stick pan to a med/low heat. It's hot enough when water drops on it, turns to beads and bounces across griddle.
5. Oil griddle very lightly and pour pancake mix into a medium round on the pan.
6. When you see bubbles forming on top, flip the cake.

Continue to lightly oil the pan every other pancake. The first 1 or 2 pancakes usually don't come out well so don't get discouraged.

Makes 8-10 pancakes, and serves a party of 4-6

**+ SOY FREE AND CAN BE MADE GLUTEN FREE
IF GLUTEN FREE FLOUR IS USED +**

Tasty Scrambled Tofu

Ingredients:

1 15-ounce block of soft tofu

½ cup vegetable broth

Spices

½ tsp black pepper

1 tbsp nutritional yeast

1½ tsp granulated garlic

1½ tsp granulated onion

1 tsp turmeric

1 tsp mustard powder

1 tsp sea salt

Vegetables

¼ cup green pepper, chopped

½ cup onion, chopped

2 cloves of garlic, chopped

3 tbsp oil, divided

1 tsp chopped fresh cilantro or parsley to taste

1 tbsp non-GMO vegan margarine, coconut or olive oil

Directions:

1. Mix the broth and the spices in a dish to make a marinade.
2. Crumble the tofu into the marinade and let sit for at least 30 minutes.
3. While the tofu is sitting, cut the veggies and sauté on a medium/low heat in 1 tbsp of oil until soft.
4. Add 2 tbsp of oil and the tofu along with the marinade to the pan and cook on a medium/ high heat.
5. Spread tofu flat in pan until bottom side is brown. Mix, spread flat again and cook until brown, about 5 minutes on each side.
6. The tofu can be cooked as long as you like by continuing to lay it flat and scramble.
7. Add 1 tbsp non GMO vegan margarine or olive oil (optional)
8. Remove from heat

Serves 4

+ GLUTEN FREE +

Tempeh Saux-sage

Dry Ingredients:

One 8 oz block of tempeh, shredded

¼ cup nutritional yeast

¼ cup spelt flour (or your favorite)

1 tbsp flax meal

1 tbsp granulated garlic, onion, whole sage

2 tsp of each, whole fennel seeds*, thyme,

basil, oregano

1 tsp black pepper

*Fennel seeds can also be ground if you

don't want them whole.

Wet Ingredients:

½ cup cold vegetable broth

2 tbsp soy sauce

1 tbsp tomato paste

1 tbsp sesame oil

1 tbsp lemon juice

Oil for frying

Directions:

1. Shred tempeh into a medium bowl.
2. Add remaining dry ingredients and mix well.
3. In a small bowl, add the wet ingredients and mix well.
4. Add the wet ingredients to dry and mix well. It may be necessary to use your hand.
5. Fill a medium size frying pan with ¼" of oil on medium heat.
6. While the oil is heating up, shape the tempeh into round ¼" patties.
7. Place patties in the oil and cook on both sides until brown about 5 minutes per side.
8. Remove from heat and place on a paper toweled plate.

Serves 4-5 **+ CAN BE MADE GLUTEN FREE IF GLUTEN FREE FLOUR IS USED +**

....

Minute Spinach

This spinach can be made any time of the day but I added it in the breakfast section because I love eating green vegetables all times of the day. This is a quick tasty way to have your greens in the morning.

Ingredients:

1 bag of spinach (about a pound)

1 tbsp minced onions

4 cloves of garlic, chopped

1 tbsp oil

½ tsp of sea salt or to taste

Directions:

1. Using a medium pan, sauté the onions and garlic in oil until soft on a low/medium heat. About 4 minutes.
2. Cut spinach into strips and add to pan along with the salt.
3. Sauté spinach in pan for one minute then remove it from the heat.
4. Continue to toss spinach in pan until wilted and immediately plate.

Serves 4

+ GLUTEN AND SOY FREE +

SOUPS

Lemongrass Coconut Soup

Ingredients:
8 oz extra firm tofu, cubed

2 tbsp oil

Pinch of sea salt

Broth:
3 lemongrass stalks cut in 1" pieces

4" ginger peeled and thinly sliced

10 peppercorns

2 cups of vegetable broth

1 whole lime plus juice cut in wedges

1 tsp sea salt

1" strip of kelp

Veggies:
4 cloves of garlic, thinly sliced

1 cup of carrots, chopped

½ cup of red onions, chopped

¼ cup of bell pepper, chopped

¼ cup of fresh green beans, chopped

¼ cup of button mushrooms, sliced (optional)

Juice of 1/2 lime

1 tbsp soy sauce

2 14oz cans of coconut milk

Directions:
1. Cut off the lower 2" from each lemongrass stalk and chop it finely. Hit the remaining stalk to bruise.
2. Add lemongrass and remaining broth ingredients to a small pot and bring to a boil.
3. Reduce heat to low and simmer for 15 minutes.
4. While the broth is simmering, begin the tofu and veggies.
5. Heat a medium pan. Add oil, tofu and salt. Sauté tofu until brown on both sides.
6. Add all veggies except mushrooms and lime. Sauté veggies until soft, about 5 minutes.
7. Add the strained broth, and remaining ingredients, except coconut milk to veggies and simmer for 15 minutes gently stirring occasionally. Add the coconut milk in the last 10 minutes
8. Ladle into bowls and serve.

Serves 6-8

+ GLUTEN FREE AND CAN BE MADE SOY FREE BY TAKING OUT TOFU AND SOY SAUCE +

A lemongrass stalk

Cut off the lower 2" from each stalk

Please hit the remaining stalk to bruise

Vegetable Miso Soup

Ingredients:

1 tbsp oil

4 oz tofu, chopped

Veggies:

1 medium onion, (1 cup) chopped

7 cloves of garlic, chopped

½ cup carrots, chopped

¾ cup green beans, chopped

6 cups of water

1 cup vegetable broth

2 tbsp soy sauce

3" strip of Kombu

3 tbsp brown miso

Directions:

1. Sauté tofu in the soup pot on a med/high heat until brown on both sides.
2. Add vegetables and sauté until soft, about 5 minutes.
3. Add water, broth, and soy sauce then bring to a boil.
4. Lower heat, add kombu and simmer for 15 minutes.
5. Turn soup off.
6. Skim off 1 cup of stock and dissolve miso into it, then add back to the soup and mix well.
7. Ladle into bowls and serve.

Serves 6-8

+ GLUTEN FREE. CAN BE MADE SOY FREE BY TAKING OUT TOFU, SOY SAUCE AND SOY MISO. USE CHICKPEA MISO AND ADD 1/4 CUP MORE OF CARROTS AND GREEN BEANS. +

Curry Lentil Soup

Ingredients:

1 cup of washed red lentils

½ cup of onion, chopped

4 cloves of garlic, chopped

2" piece of peeled ginger

1 cup cubed carrots

2 tbsp sesame or coconut oil

1 ½ cup peeled and cubed potatoes

6 cups of water

1 cup coconut milk

1 cup of diced tomatoes fresh or canned

1" strip of kelp

Juice of 1/2 lemon

Spices:

1 tbsp granulated garlic

1 tbsp granulated onion

1 tsp curry powder

½ tsp cinnamon

1 tsp sea salt

Pinch of cayenne

Directions:

1. Put lentils in a strainer and rinse them.
2. Using a medium pot or saucepan, sauté onions, garlic, ginger and carrots in oil until soft. Cook on a medium/low heat. (4 minutes).
3. Add spices and sauté for 30 seconds. Then add remaining ingredients (except kelp and lemon) and bring to a boil.
4. Reduce to a simmer, add kelp, cover and cook for 35-40 minutes, stirring occasionally.
5. Add 1 cup of water if you like your soup thinner. Remove the kelp if you choose, but it's not necessary. Lentils should be soft.
6. Squeeze in lemon juice and serve.

Serves 6-8

+ GLUTEN AND SOY FREE +

Down Home Chili

Ingredients:

3 tablespoons of oil

2 cups ground saux-sage or veggie burger

Vegetables:

1 large onion, chopped

6 cloves to 1 whole bulb garlic

1/2 cup green peppers, diced

2 medium carrots, cubed

2 cups of eggplant, peeled and cubed

Spices:

2 tsp ground coriander

2 tbsp powdered cumin

1/4 cup granulated onion

1 tbsp oregano

2 tsp basil

1/2 tsp ground fennel

1 1/2 tsp sea salt

1 tsp black pepper

One 25-oz can of red beans, drained

One 28-oz can of crushed tomatoes

1-inch piece of kombu

2 cups of water

Directions:

1. Sauté sauxsage in oil until brown.
2. Add vegetables and sauté for 5-7 minutes.
3. Add spices and cook a few minutes. Stir in beans tomatoes, and water.
4. Bring to a boil and simmer 15 minutes uncovered, stirring often. Reduce heat to low and add kombu.
5. Cover and let gently cook for a minimum of 30 minutes up to 3 hours, making sure it does not stick.
6. Chili tastes better the longer it is cooked. Adjust seasonings to your taste. Also add more water if needed • cup at a time.

Serves 6-8

SALADS

Garvey Salad

Ingredients:
1 head of romaine lettuce

Dressing:
¼ cup non-dairy mayo

8 cloves of garlic

2 tsp Dijon mustard

¼ cup olive oil

3 tbsp lemon juice

¼ tsp sea salt

¼ cup nutritional yeast

1 tsp granulated garlic

½ tsp soy sauce

1 tbsp non-dairy milk (optional)

Croutons:
4 slices of bread

1 tbsp dressing

1 tbsp olive oil

½ tsp dry rosemary

Directions:
1. Pre heat oven to 300°
2. Add all dressing ingredients to a blender and mix well.
3. For the croutons: Mix the dressing, oilive oil and rosemary then brush the mixture over one side of each slice of bread.
4. Cut the bread into medium sized cubes, place on a cookie sheet and bake for 20 minutes.
5. Tear the entire head of lettuce into bite size pieces. Wash and drain.
6. Remove the croutons from the oven and let cool for 10 minutes
7. Add ½ cup of dressing at a time to lettuce until it is as saturated as you like. Toss all ingredients together and serve.

Serves 3-4

Kale Salad

Ingredients:

4 sun-dried tomatoes

¼ cup warm water

1 lb of green kale

2 ½ tbsp toasted sesame oil

¼ cup olive oil

3 tsp granulated garlic

1 ½ - 2 tsp sea salt

The juice of ½ lemon or lime

Directions:

1. Soak tomatoes in warm water and let sit for 20 minutes until soft.
2. Cut kale in thin strips and wash.
3. Mix oils, spices (1 ½ tsp of salt) and lemon juice in a medium bowl.
4. Cut tomatoes into this strips or pieces. Add tomatoes and soaking water to oil mixture.
5. Add a little kale at a time to mixture and toss well.
6. Cover and let marinate for a minimum of 2 hours. Shake or mix every 15-20 minutes. After 2 hours taste to see if you'd like to add more salt.

Serves 4-6

+ SOY AND GLUTEN FREE ALSO ALL LIVE (RAW) EXCEPT TOASTED SESAME OIL +

Sesame Tofu Salad

Ingredients:

2 cups of tofu or saux-sage cut in thin strips

2 tbsp sesame oil

1 head of romaine or green leaf lettuce

2 tbsp shredded beets

1 tbsp red onions

1 tsp shredded ginger

½ cup of peanuts

Dash of sea salt

Dash of cayenne

Tofu Marinade:

1 tbsp peanut butter (or your favorite nut butter)

2 tbsp soy sauce

1 tsp ground ginger

1 tsp toasted sesame oil

1 tbsp granulated garlic

1 tsp granulated onions

Sesame dressing

2 tbsp lime juice

1 tbsp fresh shredded ginger

¼ cup soy sauce

3 tsp toasted sesame oil

3 tsp agave

Pinch of red pepper flakes

Directions:

1. Marinate tofu for a minimum of 30 minutes to overnight.
2. While tofu is marinating, make the dressing and set to the side.
3. Pan fry or broil tofu. Cook on both sides until brown.
4. While tofu is cooking, break lettuce into medium pieces, wash and place into a medium bowl.
5. Add tofu, dressing and remaining ingredients to the lettuce then mix.

Serves 4

+ CAN BE GLUTEN FREE IF WHEAT FREE SOY SAUCE IS USED AND IF TOFU IS USED INSTEAD OF SAUX SAGE +

Community Coleslaw

Ingredients:

8 cups of cabbage (1 medium head)

¼ cup of shredded carrots (1 medium)

Dressing:

1/3 cup agave

1 tsp sea salt

1/8 tsp pepper

½ cup non-dairy milk

½ cup non-dairy mayo

1tbsp apple cider vinegar

2 ½ tbsp lemon juice

5 dashes of hot sauce (optional)

Directions:

1. Chop the cabbage into very small pieces (about ¼ ") and place into a large bowl.

2. Then shred the carrots and mix with the cabbage.

3. Mix the dressing ingredients in a medium bowl then mix with vegetables.

4. To get the best flavor let it sit for at least 2 hours.

Serves 6   **+ GLUTEN FREE +**

Pasta-fari Salad

Ingredients:

1 package of macaroni noodles

¼ cup diced carrots

¼ cup frozen green peas or edammame

¼ cup minced onions

1/4 cup diced veggie Canadian bacon or ham (optional)

Dressing:

1 cup non-dairy mayo

¼ cup mustard

1 tbsp granulated garlic

1 tbsp granulated onion

1 tbsp dill weed

1 tsp sea salt

½ tsp black pepper to taste

1 tbsp soy sauce

Directions:

1. Follow directions on package for cooking the noodles.
2. Add carrots and green peas to pasta water and cook them along with the pasta for the last 4 minutes.
3. While food is boiling, mix together dressing ingredients in a large bowl.
4. Strain noodles and veggies. Rinse with cold water until they are fully cooled.
5. Add the noodle mix, onions and veggie bacon to the dressing then mix.
6. Let sit for at least 30 minutes.

Serves 6

+ CAN BE MADE GLUTEN FREE IF GLUTEN FREE NOODLES AND WHEAT FREE SOY SAUCE ARE USED +

My Mama's Potato Salad

Ingredients:

4 large cubed potatoes

1/3 cup of minced green pepper

¼ cup minced onion

¼ cup minced celery (1 stalk)

1 tbsp fresh parsley or 1 tsp dry

1½ tbsp mustard

½ cup relish with juice

1¼ cup non dairy mayo

¼ tsp sea salt

¼ tsp black pepper

½ tsp paprika

Directions:

1. Fill a large pot about 2/3 full with water.
2. While the water is heating, peel the potatoes.
3. Add the potatoes, cover and boil for about 35 minutes, until tender.
4. After the potatoes are finished, strain and cover with cold water for 15 minutes. This keeps the potatoes from being mushy.
5. Then cut them into bite size cubes.
6. Add all ingredients except paprika and ¼ cup of mayo.
7. Fold in ingredients until well mixed; if the salad seems dry add remaining mayo.
8. Taste and add more sea salt or pepper if needed.
9. Sprinkle the top with paprika.
10. Let sit for 30 minutes

Serves 6

+ GLUTEN FREE +

✳ VSG: A SALAD A DAY

I began the "A Salad A Day" program to help my clients incorporate more raw veggies to their diets and to help speed weight loss.

Changing your base, veggies, and protein each day enables variety of taste and nutrients. Items that should be used sparingly are for those who are working on weight loss. These foods have a large fat content.

Base: The majority of your salad should be a base. This will ensure that most of your meal will be leafy greens- a necessity for weight loss.

Vegetables: This should be the next largest portion of the salad. Use as many vegetables as you want. (daikon, radishes, and cabbage are vegetables that help remove fat). Most veggies should be raw but adding sautéed and steamed veggies gives the salad a twist.

Protein: The protein will give you energy and help you to feel full. Beans can be eaten every day along with other proteins because they are low in fat. Nuts should be used sparingly if you are trying to lose weight because they are high in fat.

Fruit: Apples and pears taste great in salad and add a nice sweet flavor. Raisins should be used sparingly because they might make you feel gassy and bloated being mixed with veggies and protein.

Spices: Use as much dry and fresh spices as you want (except salt).

Oils/Dressings: Choose dressings that are oil based instead of cream based. Ex: honey mustard, Italian, carrot ginger or salsa.
1 tablespoon of olive, flax or hemp oil can be added for extra nutrients.

Base	Carrots	Sprouts	Pumpkin seeds
Cabbage	Cabbage	Tomatoes	Sunflower seeds
Kale	Corn	Zucchini	
Lettuce	Celery		*Fruit*
Spinach	Daikon	*Protein*	Apples
	Garlic	Beans	Avocado
Vegetables	Green peas	Tofu	Pears
Asparagus	Heart of palm	Tempeh	Raisins
Artichoke hearts	Okra	Veggie Bacon	
Broccoli	Olives	Almonds	
Beets	Parsnip	Hemp seeds	
Brussel sprouts	Radishes	Nuts	
Cucumbers	Sun dried tomatoes	Peanuts	

MAIN DISHES

Savory Sauxsage Seitan

Making gluten can be a little bit of work but if you make a large amount you will be able to freeze some for later and use it as you wish.

Ingredients:

Dry

2 cups vital gluten flour

¼ cup nutritional yeast

¼ cup spelt flour

1 tbsp granulated garlic, onion, whole sage

2 tsp of each, thyme, basil, oregano and whole fennel seeds,

1 tsp black pepper

Broth

10 cups of cold water

¼ cup almond/peanut butter (optional)

1 bunch of parsley

1 whole carrot

1 celery rib

1 small onion

5 cloves of garlic

2-inch piece of kelp

Wet

1 cup cold vegetable broth

¼ cup soy sauce

¼ cup tomato paste

1 tbsp sesame oil

1 tbsp lemon juice

Directions:

1. Add the dry ingredients to a large bowl and mix. Then add the wet ingredients to a small bowl and mix well.
2. Put a hole in the center of the dry ingredients and add the wet. Mix well.
3. Knead dough for about 5 minutes. Pull into 4 or 5 patties, shaped in different sizes.
4. Add the broth ingredients and patties to a large pot and bring to a boil. Reduce the heat to medium and boil for 1 hour.
5. Let cool completely before removing seitan from the broth.
6. Remove the seitan from the broth and cut into various sizes depending on how you'd like to use it – steaks, strips, crumbled, thin slices, etc.
7. Strain the broth and discard or keep the liquid as a vegetable broth. (Broth and seitan stays fresh in the fridge for up to 5 days.)
8. They can also be frozen for later use.

1. Knead dough for 5 minutes

2. Pull into 4 or 5 patties

Serves 6

Savory Brazil Sauxsage

This is a raw version of sauxsage that can be used in nori rolls, on salads or lettuce wraps.

Ingredients:

2 cups of soaked raw brazil nuts

4 sun-dried tomatoes

4 cloves of garlic

¼ cup minced onions

2 tsp olive oil

Spices:

1 tsp of each: fennel seeds, granulated garlic and dry basil

2 tsp of each: sea salt and dry whole sage

1/2 tsp of black pepper

Directions:

1. Soak the brazil nuts at least 4 hour to overnight and strain.
2. Soak the sun-dried tomatoes in warm water for at least 30 minutes and strain.
3. Lightly pulse the nuts and tomatoes (not the soaking water) in a food processor until chopped.
4. Add the remaining ingredients until it becomes fluffy and crumbled.

Serves 6

+ GLUTEN FREE, SOY FREE AND LIVE (RAW) +

Pepper Steak

Ingredients:

1 lb of extra firm tofu (or sauxsage).

Veggies

½ cup of oil
4 cloves of garlic, chopped
2 tbsp fresh ginger, chopped
1/3 cup green pepper, cut in strips
1/3 cup red pepper, cut in strips
1/3 cup yellow peppers, cut in strips
1/3 cup onions, cut in strips
1/3 cup celery, cut in strips
1 cup broccoli, chopped
½ cup of tomatoes, chopped

Marinade / Sauce

¼ cup vegetable broth
¼ cup soy sauce
2 tsp granulated garlic
2 tsp granulated onion
1 tsp ground ginger
Pinch of red pepper flakes

Directions:

1. Mix together marinade in a small bowl or cup.
2. Cut tofu into nuggets or cubes (see page 153). Marinate it making sure all pieces are soaked marinade for a minimum of 30 minutes.
3. Heat a medium wok or pan. After pan is hot, add oil, then immediately add tofu to prevent splattering.
4. Fry tofu in oil on a medium high heat, until firm and browned on both sides.
5. Add all veggies except for the tomatoes and sauté for 5- 8 minutes until tender.
6. Add sauce and tomatoes, cook for 2-3 minutes.
7. Serve with rice.

Serves 4

+ CAN BE MADE GLUTEN FREE IF WHEAT FREE SOY SAUCE AND TOFU IS USED +

Buffalo Tofu

Ingredients:

1 15oz block of extra firm tofu, frozen and thawed

Marinade:

¼ cup peanut butter

1 tbsp soy sauce

2 tbsp nutritional yeast

1 cup vegetable both

Oil for frying

Wet batter:

1 cup of spelt flour

2 tsp of baking powder

½ tsp sea salt

1 cup of non-dairy milk

½ cup of coconut milk

1 tbsp of agave or honey

Dry batter:

2 cups spelt flour

2 tsp granulated garlic

2 tsp sea salt

Hot sauce:

¼ cup of non GMO vegan margarine, melted

2-5 tbsp of hot sauce

2 tbsp apple cider vinegar

Celery, carrot sticks and ranch dressing

Directions:

1. Press water out of tofu and cut into nugget size pieces (see page 153).
2. Mix all marinade ingredients in a bowl then add the tofu. Cover the tofu well with marinade and let sit for 1 hr to overnight.
3. While the tofu is marinating, combine the hot sauce ingredients in a small pan, cook on low for 3-5 min. Sit to the side.
4. In a plate, add dry batter ingredients.
5. Fill a frying pan with 2" of oil. Heat on medium/high heat.
6. Add wet batter ingredients to a bowl and mix well. Batter should be thick and runny. Add dry batter ingredients to a bowl and mix well.
7. Dip tofu in wet batter, covering all sides, then immediately add to the dry batter.
8. Lightly shake off any excess flour and add tofu to the pan. Cook until brown on both sides then drain on paper towels.
9. After all tofu has been cooked, pour hot sauce over and serve immediately with vegetables.

Serves 5

+ CAN BE MADE GLUTEN FREE IF WHEAT FREE SOY SAUCE & GLUTEN FREE FLOUR IS USED +

Southern Fried Tofu

Ingredients:

1 15 ounce block of frozen and thawed extra firm tofu

½ cup flour

2 tbsp soy sauce

1 tbsp oil

Oil for frying

Spices: 1 tsp each: chili powder, oregano, italian seasoning, parsley, granulated garlic, thyme, and pinch of black pepper or cayenne.

Directions:

1. Press water out of tofu and cut into strips. (see page 153).
2. In a small bowl, blend spices with soy sauce and tbsp of oil. *Add spices to flour at the same time.
3. Pour marinade on tofu and rub into both sides of each piece, set aside. (Let tofu marinate for 30 minutes – overnight.)
4. Fill a frying pan with 2" of oil. Heat on medium/high heat
5. Dredge tofu in flour and add to heated oil.
6. Pan fry each side for 4 minutes.
7. Drain on paper towel or brown paper bag.

Serves a party of 4

+ CAN BE MADE GLUTEN FREE IF WHEAT FREE SOY SAUCE AND GLUTEN FREE FLOUR IS USED +

Chimichanga

Ingredients:

1 15 ounce block of extra firm tofu frozen and thawed or 2 cups of gluten

6-8 whole grain tortillas at room temperature

Fresh spinach

Black or green olives

Basic brown rice

Oil for frying

Marinade for tofu or sauxsage:

4 cloves of minced garlic

2 tbsp chili powder

1 tsp oregano

1 tsp cumin

1 tsp granulated onion

1 tbsp paprika

1/8 tsp ground cloves

¼ tsp sea salt

-continued on next page-

Beans

1 can of black beans

¼ tsp cumin

¼ tsp granulated onion

¼ tsp granulated garlic

2 tbsp crushed tomatoes (or salsa)

Pinch of sea salt

Veggies

1 tbsp oil

¼ cup of chopped green pepper

¼ cup of minced onion

2 cloves of minced garlic

1 tbsp canned green chilies (mild or hot)

Directions:

1. Press the water out of tofu and crumble.
2. Mix the marinade ingredients in a medium bowl that has a lid.
3. Add tofu/gluten to marinade. Cover and shake. Then let sit for 30 minutes to overnight.
4. While the tofu is marinating, add the beans and its ingredients to a small pot.
   Simmer on low, stirring occasionally until the remaining ingredients are done.
5. Heat a frying pan on medium/high. Fill the pan with 1" of oil and the tofu/gluten.
   Sauté until brown. Add remaining vegetables and sauté for a few more minutes until soft.
6. Meanwhile, heat oven to 350°, wrap tortillas in foil and let warm for about 10 minutes.
7. Add tofu, beans, rice, spinach, and olives to a tortilla. Fold envelope style then wrap.
8. Fill a heavy skillet or saucepan with 1" of oil, and heat on med/high.
9. Carefully place wrap, fold side down into oil and fry on both sides until brown, about 1 minute, Fry 2 at a time.

Serves 6-8

Tofu-tater wrap

Ingredients:

1 15 ounce block of extra firm tofu frozen
and thawed
3 tbsp oil (divided)
1 tbsp soy sauce
¼ cup of vegetable broth

1 ½ large potatoes cut in ¼" oval rounds
2 tbsp oil

4 large tortillas
Fresh spinach or lettuce
Sliced tomatoes
Sliced onions
Non-dairy mayo or tofu cream cheese

Spices:

1 tsp sea salt
3 tsp granulated garlic
3 tsp granulated onion
1 tsp lemon pepper

Dijon soy dressing

1 tbsp of olive oil
1 tbsp Dijon mustard
2 tbsp soy sauce

Directions:

1. Mix the spices together in a small cup.
2. Cut the tofu into steaks (see page 153) and place in a bowl for marinating.
3. Add the soy sauce, vegetable broth, and 2-3 tsps of the spice mix to the tofu and let marinate while cooking potatoes or overnight.
4. Make the dressing and sit to the side.
5. Slice potatoes and sprinkle both sides with the spice mix.
6. Heat a frying pan to a medium heat then add 1 tbsp of oil and potatoes. Brown on both sides and remove from the pan.
7. Add 2 tbsp of oil then add tofu to pan. Brown on both sides, cooking the tofu well done.
8. While the tofu is cooking, sit the tortillas on top of the tofu to heat them or heat them lightly on both sides after the tofu is done.
9. Layer each tortilla with the mayo, potatoes, tofu, tomatoes, spinach onions and dressing.
10. Fold the tortillas and lay flat in the frying pan. Brown on both sides.

★ *Tip:* Salsa or bbq sauce are other dressing options for the wrap.
This wrap can also be cooked on a grill instead of pan fried.

Serves 4

+ CAN BE MADE GLUTEN FREE IF WHEAT FREE SOY SAUCE AND GLUTEN FREE TORTILLAS ARE USED +

Creole Red Beans and Rice

Ingredients:
7 cups water

1 cup vegetable broth

2 cups dry or frozen beans (red, butter or lima)

Rue:
1 tbsp flour

2 tbsp oil

Veggies
2 tbsp oil

½ cup green pepper

1 cup onions

½ cup carrots

½ cup celery

3 cloves garlic

Spices
2 bay leaves

1½ tbsp granulated garlic

1½ tbsp granulated onion

1 tsp pepper

2 bay leaves

1 strip of kelp

2 tsp salt

Directions:
1. If you are using dry beans, soak them overnight, then strain.
2. Heat a large pot on medium/low heat. Add oil and flour from the rue and sauté until brown, about 5 minutes.
3. Add the vegetable broth to mix the rue then add the remaining ingredients except the salt.
4. If you are using dry beans, cook them for 3 to 4 hours. If you are using frozen beans, cook them for 45 minutes to 1 hour.
5. Add the salt during the last 30 minutes of cooking for dry beans and during the last 10 minutes for the frozen.
6. Serve over rice.

Serves a party of 6-8

+ SOY FREE. CAN BE MADE GLUTEN FREE IF GLUTEN FREE FLOUR IS USED +

Daal

Ingredients:

1 cup of red lentils

2 cups of water

1 tbsp of oil

1/2 cup of onions

6 cloves of garlic

2" piece of ginger

1 cup vegetable broth

¾ cup tomatoes

1" strip of Kombu

Juice of ½ lime or lemon

Spices:

½ tsp of ground coriander

½ tsp turmeric

½ tsp granulated garlic

¾ tsp chili powder

1 tsp sea salt

Directions:

1. Wash lentils and drain.
2. Add water and lentils to a saucepan.
3. Bring to a boil. Reduce heat to medium/low add the kombu and simmer for 10 minutes uncovered until most of the water is dissolved.
4. While lentils are simmering, add oil, onions, ginger and garlic to another pan and sauté until tender, about 3-5 minutes.
5. Add spices, except sea salt, to veggies and sauté for 30 seconds.
6. Add vegetable broth and tomatoes to veggies making sure you get all the spices out of pan.
7. Add broth and veggie mix to the lentils. Cover and simmer on a medium/low heat for 15 minutes, stirring occasionally. Keep a close eye on lentils in the last 5 minutes making sure they do not stick.
8. Add salt, lime and you can add ½ cup more water if you'd like the lentils more watery.

Serves a party of 4-6

+ SOY FREE AND GLUTEN FREE +

Sauxsage Pizza

Ingredients

Toppings:

1 cup ground sauxsage
(or ground veggie burgers)
2 tbsp of oil
½ cup onions
½ cup green peppers
½ cup mushrooms
½ cup pineapples
Or your favorite pizza toppings

Motza cheese (see page 150) or your
favorite nondairy cheese
Pizza dough (see page 134)
Corn meal for dusting pan

Sauce:

1½ cups tomato puree
1 tsp oregano (dried)
1 tsp basil (dried)
1 tsp granulated garlic
1 tsp agave
½ tsp sea salt
¼ tsp black pepper

Fully cover crust with
cheez sauce

Directions:

1. Before you heat the oven, set one oven rack on the top row and the other in the middle of the oven. Preheat oven to broil.
2. Spread cornmeal over a pizza pan or cookie sheet and set to the side.
3. Sauté sauxsage until brown.
4. While the sauxsage is sautéing, mix the sauce ingredients in a bowl.
5. Roll out pizza dough in a 10-inch round and place on pan. Pinch around the edge of the dough to make the crust end.
6. Spread sauce evenly around pie then drizzle cheez over sauce.
7. Place the pizza on the top rack in the oven and cook for 5-7 minutes. The cheez should begin to bubble a little.
8. While the cheez is browning, cut and prepare your toppings.
9. Remove the crust from the oven and sprinkle toppings evenly around.
10. Bake for 10-15 minutes depending on how crispy you like your crust.
11. Take out and slice.

Topping options: olives, corn, broccoli, spinach, banana peppers, sun dried tomatoes, lettuce and avocados. Add lettuce and avocadoes after the pizza is cooked

Quick pizza option: use a frozen pizza crust, hamburger buns or pita bread as crust.

Serves 4-6

Crispy Fried Cauliflower

Ingredients:

1 head of cauliflower

Sea salt and pepperr

Wet batter:

1 cup of spelt or wheat flour

1 cup of non-dairy milk

½ cup of coconut milk

1 tsp of baking powder

1 tbsp of agave

½ tsp sea salt

1 tsp chili powder

Dry batter:

2 cups spelt or wheat flour

2 tsp granulated garlic

1 tbsp nutritional yeast

2 tsp sea salt

1/2 tsp chili powder

1 tbsp arrowroot or cornstarch

Directions:

1. Mix together the dry batter and put in a paper bag.
2. Then mix the wet batter together in a medium bowl.
3. Heat a large pan on a medium/high heat. Add the oil.
4. While the pan is heating, cut the cauliflower into medium pieces, wash and drain, then sprinkle with sea salt and pepper.
5. Dip about a ½ cup of cauliflower in the wet batter, making sure all sides are covered and drop each one into the bag.
6. Shake the bag until the cauliflower is covered and put enough pieces in the pan to fill it but do not overcrowd.
7. Cook, turning on both sides until golden brown.
8. Drain on a paper towel and serve.

Serves 5

+ SOY FREE AND CAN BE MADE GLUTEN FREE IF USING GLUTEN FREE FLOUR +

SIDES: VEGGIES

Al Greens

The cooking time on the greens depends on how you prefer them. They will be lighter, less tender, but will retain more vitamins the less they are cooked. The longer they are cooked, the more tender they will be. If you are using a larger bunch, double the ingredients.

Ingredients:

2 tbsp oil

5 cloves garlic

¼ cup onions, chopped

1 cup tomatoes, diced

1 pound of greens (collard, kale or chard), washed and chopped

1 cup water

1 cup vegetable broth

2 tsp garlic powder

1 tbsp soy sauce

Pinch of black pepper or cayenne

1 tsp sea salt or to taste

Directions:

1. Stack greens and cut off stems.
2. Roll stack of greens and cut into thin shreds about ¼"- ½" thick
3. Wash in a strainer until fully cleaned.
4. Sauté garlic and onion in oil on medium/low heat until soft, 3-5 minutes.
5. Add tomatoes and greens, sauté for 5 minutes.
6. Add water, vegetable broth, garlic powder, soy sauce and pepper.
7. Cook for 15-20 minutes, cover, stirring occasionally. Add sea salt to taste.

See step 1

See step 2

Serves 4

See step 2

+ GLUTEN FREE AND CAN BE MADE SOY FREE IF SOY SAUCE IS OMITTED +

Coconut Collards

Ingredients

1 tbsp of oil

3 medium carrots, chopped

½ cup chopped onions

3 cloves of garlic

1 lb of collard greens

1 can of coconut milk

1 cup of vegetable broth

Spices:

2 tsp granulated garlic

2 tsp granulated onion

½ tsp ground ginger

¼ tsp red pepper flakes

1 tsp sea salt

Directions:

1. Wash and cut greens into small strips.
2. Heat a medium pot on low and add oil, carrots, onions and garlic then sauté for 3-5 minutes until soft.
3. Add spices and sauté for 30 seconds, and then add greens.
4. Add remaining ingredients and cover.
5. Simmer greens on a medium/low heat for 15-20 minutes, stirring occasionally.

Serves 4

+ SOY FREE AND GLUTEN FREE +

Place a small amount of filling on the lower 2/3 of the wrap. Be careful not to add so much that it will not be able to fully close.

Roll the wrap over once and fold the corners in.

Continue to roll the wrap and seal closed with a little water.

Crispy Collard Green Rolls

Ingredients
2 cups leftover collard greens, chopped small (see page 111)

1 veggie hot dog, minced (optional)

1 tsp oil

Spring roll wrappers

Water

Enough oil to fill 1 inch of pan

Spices:
2 tsp granulated garlic

2 tsp granulated onion

2 tsp ground ginger

¼ tsp red pepper flakes

½ tsp sea salt

Directions:
1. Sauté dogs in tsp of oil until lightly brown. Remove from heat and mix with greens.
2. Heat frying oil on medium high heat.
3. Roll green mixture in 2 sheets of spring roll paper
4. Fry rolls until golden brown on both sides

Serves 6

+ CAN BE SOY FREE IF HOT DOGS ARE OMITTED +

Pz & Cz

Ingredients:

1 tbsp of oil

2 ½ large carrots chopped

2 cups of green peas, fresh or frozen

2 tbsp minced onions

¼ cup of vegetable broth

1 tbsp of non GMO vegan margarine

(optional)

Spices:

1 tsp granulated garlic

½ tsp sea salt

¼ tsp black pepper

½ tsp dill

Directions:

1. Warm a medium size pan on a medium/low heat.
2. Wash and chop carrots then add oil and carrots to the pan and sauté for 5 minutes.
3. Add peas, broth, spices and margarine. Cover and simmer for 5 more minutes.
4. Cook until tender and serve.

Serves 4

+ SOY AND GLUTEN FREE +

B-Sprouts

Ingredients

1 lb of brussel sprouts (smaller ones are more tender)

1 tbsp + 2tsps coconut oil or favorite vegetable oil (divided)

4 cloves of garlic

1/3 cup vegetable broth

1 ½ tsp granulated garlic

½- 1 tsp salt

¼ tsp black pepper

Directions:

1. Cut brussel sprouts in half and wash.
2. Heat a large pan on low; add 1 tbsp oil and sauté garlic for 3 minutes.
3. Increase heat to medium, add brussel sprouts, toss with oil and garlic then lay flat for 5 minutes. They may brown slightly.
6. Add broth and spices, toss then lay sprouts flat again.
7. Cover and simmer for 8 minutes. Most of broth should be cooked out.
8. Uncover and cook 5 more minutes. Add 2 tbsps of oil or non-GMO vegan margarine at the end. Serve.

Serves 4   **+ SOY AND GLUTEN FREE +**

Coup de Grille Veggies

Ingredients

2 cups carrots

2 cups green beans

2 cups small red potatoes

¼ cup oil

1 cup veggie broth or as much as needed

Spices:

1 tbsp each: granulated garlic and granulated onion

1 tsp each: thyme and sea salt

½ tsp black pepper

Pinch of cayenne

Directions:

1. Cut the carrots in about 3-inch sticks. Cut the ends of the green beans then cut them in half. Cut the potatoes in quarters.
2. Place the veggies side by side in a pan that can fit on your grill.
3. Mix the 1 cup veggie broth, oil and spices in a cup or bowl then pour over the veggies.
4. Cover the vegetables then put on a hot grill. Cook for 20-30 minutes, checking every 8 minutes making sure nothing is sticking. If veggies stick add ½ cup of vegetable broth at a time and use a spatula to loosen them.
5. Uncover for the last 8 minutes.

Serves 5-6

+ SOY AND GLUTEN FREE +

Gold Grilled Corn

Ingredients

6 ears of corn with husks

Oil or non GMO vegan margarine

Spices:

1 tsp each: sea salt, chili powder, paprika, garlic powder

Pinch of cayenne

Directions:

1. Keep the husk on the corn and place on a warm grill.
2. Turn every 5-7 minutes depending on how hot the grill is. It's okay if the husks burn some.
3. Cook for 25-30 minutes until done.
4. Unpeel the husks and top with spices and oil.

Serves 4-6

+ SOY AND GLUTEN FREE +

Classic Corn on the Cob

Ingredients

4 ears of corn

8-10 cups of water

Half of a lime ***

2 tsp oil

Spices:

1 tbsp each: granulated garlic powder, granulated and chili powder

1 tsp each: thyme and sea salt

½ tsp black pepper

Pinch of cayenne

Directions:

1. Add water to a large pot and bring to a boil
2. Remove husk from corn and break cob in half.
3. Squeeze the juice of the lime into the pot and add the lime.
3. Add remaining ingredients to pot.
4. Turn heat to medium/high, lightly boil for 20 minutes.

★ *Tip:* Adding lime to corn releases the B vitamins and makes it more absorbable to the body. Indigenous people of the Americas (Native Americans) also practiced this cooking technique.

Serves 4-6

+ SOY AND GLUTEN FREE +

Mouth Waterin' Butternut Squash

Ingredients:

1 large butternut squash

1/3 cup 100 % maple syrup or honey

1 tbsp molasses

1 tsp cinnamon

1 tbsp of oil or non-GMO veggie margarine

Directions:

1. Preheat oven to 425°.

2. Cut the squash in half, separating the round bottom from the long end, using a large knife. The shell may be hard so it will take a little muscle to get open.

3. Spoon out the seeds and cut the entire squash into chunks and place in a baking dish.

4. Mix the molasses, maple syrup and cinnamon in a small cup or bowl then pour over the squash.

5. Evenly distribute the margarine on top of the squash

6. Cover and bake for 25 minutes until soft.

7. Then uncover and cook for 10 more minutes to dry it out some.

★ *Tip:* this can also be cooked on the grill.

Serves 4

+ SOY AND GLUTEN FREE +

Can't Belive This is Squash

Ingredients

1 med kabocha squash

1/3 cup maple syrup or honey

½ tsp molasses

1 tsp cinnamon

1 tbsp of oil or non-GMO veggie margarine

Kabocha Squash

Directions:

1. Preheat oven to 400°.
2. Cut the squash in half using a large knife. The shell is very hard so it will take a little muscle to get open.
3. Spoon out the seeds and cut the squash into chunks and place in a baking dish.
4. Mix the molasses, maple syrup and cinnamon in a small cup or bowl then pour over the squash.
5. Cover and bake for 30 minutes until soft. Then uncover and bake 10 more minutes to dry the squash out.

Serves 5-6

+ SOY AND GLUTEN FREE +

Yams Sweet Yam

Ingredients:

3 medium yams (red garnet) cut in chunks

½ cup maple syrup or agave (or more if you like them sweeter)

1 tsp cinnamon

½ cup water

1 tbsp of oil or Non GMO veggie margarine

Directions:

1. Preheat oven to 400°.
2. You can peel the yams first, but I usually don't. Cut yams into 1" thick chunks and place in a baking dish.
3. Mix the water, maple syrup, oil and cinnamon in a small cup or bowl then pour over the yams.
4. Cover and bake at 400° for 30-35 minutes, until soft.

Serves 4

+ SOY AND GLUTEN FREE +

Mashem' up

Ingredients

8-10 cups of water

8 medium red, white or yellow potatoes

1 tsp granulated garlic

1/3 cup vegan margarine or olive oil

1 cup non-dairy milk

1½ tsp sea salt

½ tsp black pepper

Directions:

1. Bring water to a boil.
2. Peel the potatoes, cut into cubes and wash.
3. Add the potatoes to the boiling water and cook for 20 minutes or until soft enough to easily stick a knife through it.
4. Drain the potatoes and add them back to the pot.
5. Then add garlic, margarine, sea salt, pepper, and a 1/2 cup of almond milk.
6. Mash the potatoes or use hand blender to mix.
7. Add more milk if necessary.

Serves 5

+ SOY AND GLUTEN FREE +

Oven Roasted Sweet potato fries

Ingredients:

2 medium sweet potatoes with skin

2 tbsp oil

½ tsp coriander

½ tsp chili powder

½ tsp granulated garlic

½ tsp paprika

½ tsp sea salt

Directions:

1. Place one oven rack in the 2nd from the top slot and place another rack in the 2nd from the bottom slot.
2. Preheat oven to 450°.
3. Cover a cookie sheet with parchment paper or foil and sit to the side.
4. Wash and slice potatoes into ¼ inch strips.
5. Mix the oil and spices in a small bowl or cup and pour over the potatoes and mix well.
6. Lay the potatoes flat on the sheet and put it on the 2nd rack from the bottom in the oven. Bake for 20 minutes.
7. Switch the sheet to the 2nd rack from the top and cook for 10 more minutes.

Cut potatoes in 1/4 inch strips

Serves 4

+ SOY AND GLUTEN FREE +

Brooklyn Fried Plantains

Ingredients

2 ripe plantains

Enough oil for frying

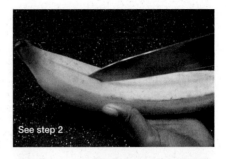

See step 2

Directions:

1. Fill a medium frying pan 1/3 full with oil. Heat on a medium high heat.
2. Slice only the skin of the plantain lengthwise to remove the peel from the fruit.
3. Remove the peel and slice the plantain in 1 inch diagonal pieces.
4. Fry the plantains on both sides until they turn golden brown.
5. Drain plantains on a paper towel or brown paper bag.

See step 3

Serves 4

+ SOY AND GLUTEN FREE +

See step 3

Sweet Baked Beans

Ingredients

5 cans (of 4 ½ cups frozen) of cannelloni (or small white) beans

¾ cup of diced onions

6 rosemary springs

A drizzle of sesame oil

Sauce:

½ cup molasses

1 cup ketchup

¼ cup mustard

½ tsp black pepper

1 tsp sea salt

¼ cup of maple syrup

1 cup of water

Directions:

1. Mix sauce ingredients together in a small bowl.
2. Put beans, rosemary and onions in a pan and mix well. Then pour the sauce on top.
3. Let the beans sit in the sauce 4 hours. The longer they sit, the better they taste. Letting them marinate overnight is best.
4. When they are ready to go in preheat oven to 350°. Then drizzle about 2 tbsp of sesame oil on top.
5. Cover and bake for 25 minutes.

★ *Tip:* This can also be cooked on the grill.

Serves 8

+ SOY AND GLUTEN FREE +

SIDES: GRAINS

Brown Pride Rice

Ingredients:

1 cup brown rice

2 cups water

1 vegetable bullion cube

1 tsp oil

¼ tsp sea salt

1" strip of kelp

Directions:

1. Wash the rice. (see below)
2. Add all ingredients to pot except kelp and bring to a boil.
3. Reduce heat to low/medium, add kelp, then cover.
4. Simmer for 45 minutes. (DO NOT REMOVE COVER.)
5. After 45 minutes, remove from heat. Let stand 5 minutes.
6. Take cover off and fluff with fork.

★ *Tip:* 1 tsp of turmeric can be added to make yellow rice

Serves 4

+ **SOY AND GLUTEN FREE** +

Washing Rice

1. Soak rice over night or rinse well until water runs clear.

Cinnamon Coconut Cous Cous

Ingredients

1½ cup water

½ cup coconut milk, fresh or canned

1 cup cous cous

¼ cup shredded unsweetened coconut

Spices:

1/8 tsp cinnamon

1 tsp sea salt

1 tsp coconut oil

Directions:

1. Bring water and coconut milk to a boil in a small pot.

2. Add cous cous, oil and spices.

3. Turn heat off and cover.

4. Let stand for 5 minutes.

5. Add shredded coconut and fluff with a fork.

Serves 4

+ SOY FREE +

Fried Rice

Ingredients:

3 cups cooked brown pride rice
(see page 125)

1 tbsp oil

¼ cup diced onions

¼ cup diced carrots

¼ cup diced celery

¼ cup corn kernels

¼ cup diced green peas

1/3 cup bean sprouts (optional)

1" piece of ginger

¼-1/3 cup Bragg's liquid amino's

Directions:

1. Using a medium wok or pan, sauté onions, carrots, celery, and corn in oil until soft. Cook on a medium heat, about 5 minutes.
2. Turn heat up to high.
3. Add remaining vegetables and rice and sauté for 3 minutes.
4. Add Braggs and fry 2 more minutes. Cook longer if desired.

Serves 4

+ SOY AND GLUTEN FREE +

....

Mo Millet

Ingredients

1 ½ cups millet

1 cup coconut milk

2 ¼ cup water

¼ cup diced onions

1/3 cup diced celery (about 1 stalk)

2 cloves diced garlic

1" kombu seaweed

Spices:

2 tsp granulated garlic

1 tsp sea salt

½ tsp cumin

½ tsp black pepper

Directions:

1. Soak millet for 5-30 min. wash then strain
2. While millet is soaking cut the onions, celery and garlic.
3. Add all ingredients to a pot except seaweed. Bring to a boil.
4. Turn the heat down to a medium/low heat, add seaweed and cover.
5. Cook for 20 minutes. Immediately fluff with a fork and let stand for 5-10 minutes.

Serves 4   **+ SOY AND GLUTEN FREE +**

Wache

Ingredients

1 cup black eyed peas, canned or frozen

1 tbsp oil

1/2 cup each: onions, carrots, and green peppers

2 cloves of garlic

1 tsp each: coriander, thyme, and sea salt

3/4 cup water

1 ½ cup veggie broth

1 cup brown rice

1-inch piece of kombu

Directions:

1. Wash the rice and strain. (See page 125)
2. Dice onions, green pepper, carrots, and garlic.
3. Using a medium pot, add oil and veggies and sauté on a medium/low heat until soft, about 5 minutes.
4. Add spices and salt sauté for 30 seconds.
5. Add remaining ingredients except for kombu. Bring to a boil. Turn down heat to low/medium. Add kombu and cover.
6. Let simmer for 50 minutes. Do not remove the lid until done.
7. Remove from heat, let stand for 5 minutes. Fluff with fork.

Serves 4-6

+ SOY AND GLUTEN FREE +

Cornbread Dressing

Ingredients:

1 whole cornbread (see page 131)

Seasonings:

¼ cup each, chopped: onions, green peppers, celery, carrots, mushrooms

2 cloves garlic

1 tbsp oil

Spices:

1 tbsp each: parsley, granulated garlic, flax meal,

2 tbsp sage

1 tsp thyme

½ tbsp oregano

¼ tsp black pepper

1 tsp sea salt

Wet:

2 cups of mushroom broth* (divided)

1 cup almond milk

¼ cup veggie broth

Directions:

Preheat oven to 400 degrees.

1. Sauté seasoning in oil for 5 minutes.

2. Crumble cornbread into a large bowl. Add spices. Mix well.

3. Add seasonings, almond milk, vegetable broth and 1 cup of mushroom broth. Let stand for 5 minutes to test moistness. The dressing should be moist, but not soupy. If it's too dry, add half of the remaining a little at a time until you have reached desired consistency.

4. Pour into a lightly oiled 9-inch round pan, cover.

5. Bake at 400 degrees for 45 minutes to 1 hour. It's ready when the edges around the pan and the top begin to brown.

★ *Tip: During the Holla days sometimes you may be able to find a vegan creamy mushroom soup. Use this if you can find it.*

Serves 6-8

+ SOY FREE AND CAN BE GLUTEN FREE IF GLUTEN FREE FLOUR IS USED IN THE CORNBREAD +

Mac- N- Cheez

Ingredients:

1 16-oz package of brown rice elbow noodles

2 tsp flour

1 tsp black pepper

2 tsp sea salt

1 cup of nutritional yeast

1/4 coconut oil or oil of your choice

2 1/4 cups of almond milk or your favorite non-dairy milk

3 slices of vegan rice cheddar cheese (or your favorite non dairy cheese)

3 slices of vegan rice pepper jack or mozzarella cheese (or your favorite non dairy cheese)

Directions:

Preheat oven to 350 degrees.

1. Boil noodles for 10 minutes, strain. They should be aldente.

2. While the noodles are cooking, mix all of the ingredients together except the cheese.

3. Stack 3 slices of the cheese and dice them, then loosen then up so they do not stick.
   Repeat with the other 3 slices.

4. Put the noodles in the 9"x13" pan and add the wet mixture and mix well.

5. Next add the diced cheese to the noodles and mix well.

6. Cover the noodles and bake for 15 minutes. Then uncover and bake for 15 more minutes.

7. When it's done, you may need to lightly mix the noodles for the cheese to melt.

Serves 6-8

+ SOY FREE AND CAN BE GLUTEN FREE IF GLUTEN FREE FLOUR IS USED +

BREADS & DESSERTS

Country Corn Bread

Ingredients

Dry

1 cup flour

1 cup of cornmeal

2 tsp baking powder

1 tbsp flax seed meal

Wet

1/3 cup of non-GMO margarine

¼ cup agave or honey

1¼ cup almond milk

Directions:

Preheat oven to 350°.

1. Oil a 9" cast iron skillet and lightly flour. Set aside, (see page 145) for flour instructions.

 2. Put dry ingredients into a large bowl. Mix well.

3. Cream margarine with a hand mixer or large wooden spoon. Add agave and mix with margarine. Then add milk. Mix well.

4. Add wet ingredients to dry and mix well.

5. Pour batter into pan and bake for 20-25 minutes, until fork or toothpick poked in the middle comes out clean.

6. Let cool for 5-10 minutes

Serves 6-8

+ SOY FREE AND CAN BE GLUTEN FREE IF GLUTEN FREE FLOUR IS USED. IF MAKING GLUTEN FREE BAKE FOR 10-15 MINUTES +

Hush Pups

Ingredients

Dry:

2 cups corn meal

1 tsp baking powder

½ tsp baking soda

1 tsp salt

1 tbsp flax seed meal

Dash of cayenne

½ tsp garlic powder

½ tsp onion powder

Wet:

1 tbsp agave

1 ¼ cup non-dairy milk

¼ cup finely chopped green onions

2 tbsp yellow onion

Enough oil to fry

Directions:

1. Mix all dry ingredients in a bowl.
2. Mix all wet ingredients in a separate bowl.
3. Mix the wet and dry together. Batter should be moist but not runny.
4. Fill a medium pan with 1 ½ inch of oil and heat on a medium high heat.
5. Shape hush puppies into balls and fry on both sides until golden brown.
6. Drain on a paper towel.

Shape the batter into balls

Serves a party of 6-8

+ SOY AND GLUTEN FREE +

East Indian Roti

Ingredients

1 ¼ cup of flour

1 tsp sea salt

1 tsp agave

¼ cup oil

½ cup non dairy milk (room temperature)

Directions:

1. Sift flour and salt into a bowl.
2. Add agave, oil and milk a little at a time and knead the dough enough to make a soft smooth dough.
3. Cover with plastic wrap and leave for 2 hours or overnight.
4. Divide into 8 equal parts and shape into balls.
5. Add a little oil to half of your worktop and a little flour to the other half.
6. Flatten a ball with a rolling pin (on oiled surface) and fold in ½ tsp of oil.
7. Roll up dough and twist it into a coil, pressing one open end onto the top.
8. Flatten it again as thin as possible into a round shape.
9. Beginning at one of the open ends, roll up dough tightly and coil it again as before.
10. Flatten dough (1/4") slowly onto lightly floured surface as before to make one roti skin.
11. Repeat steps 5-10 for the remaining balls. Keep skins covered until you begin cooking.
12. Heat a pan and add a small amount of oil.
13. Cook individually over a medium/low heat turning until brown on both sides. (Cook each side about 45 seconds.)

Serves a party of 8

+ SOY FREE +

See steps 5 & 6

See step 6

Fold the oil into the dough

Roll the dough into a strip

Twist into a coil

Press the open end onto the top

Traditional Pizza Dough

Ingredients

1 cup warm water (about 110° F)

1 tsp agave or sweetener

1 envelope of active dry yeast

2¾ cups of spelt or whole wheat flour

2 tbsp flax seed meal

1 tsp sea salt

2 tbsp non dairy milk

1½ tbsp olive oil

Fine cornmeal for dusting

Directions:

1. In a small bowl, add agave and yeast to warm water, stir with fork until yeast and agave dissolve. Let stand until foamy about 5 minutes.
2. In a food processor or bowl, pulse (mix) flour, flax and salt to combine.
3. Add in the milk, oil and yeast mixture to the flour. Pulse until mixture comes together but is still slightly sticky. Dough should pull away cleanly from your fingers after it is squeezed.
4. Turn dough onto a lightly floured surface and knead for 1 minute until a smooth ball forms.
5. Place dough in a lightly oiled bowl, smooth side up, cover with plastic wrap and let rise in a warm place until doubled in size, about 40-60 minutes.
6. Punch dough down onto a lightly floured work surface and cut in half.
7. Return 1 ball to oiled bowl and cover. Pat remaining ball into a flattened disk.
8. Using your hands or a rolling pin, stretch or press dough into desired shape.
9. Sprinkle pizza pan or cookie sheet with cornmeal and lay the crust on the pan.
10. Top with pizza ingredients. Bake.

Makes 2- 12" pizzas

+ SOY FREE +

NY Pizza Dough (no yeast)

Ingredients

Dry

2 cups of flour

2 tbsp flax seed meal

1 tsp salt

2 tsp baking powder

½ tsp Italian seasoning (or oregano)

1 tsp garlic powder

2 tsp baking soda

Wet

2 tsp agave

1¼ cup milk

4 tbsp of oil (divided)

Directions:

Preheat oven to 400°.

1. In a large bowl, add dry ingredients and mix.
2. In a small bowl, add wet ingredients, 2 tbsp of oil and mix.
3. Make a hole into the dry ingredients and add the wet.
4. Mix dough with hand and knead for about 2 minutes.
5. Roll into a ball. The dough will be sticky. Cut in half.
6. Place one ball onto a well floured surface. Roll it with a rolling pin to 1/2 " thick, flipping the crust over and re flouring the surface as needed.
7. Lay the dough on pan and pinch the edges around to make the crust.
8. Spread or brush 2 tablespoon of oil onto crust so the sauce won't soak in.
9. Top with pizza ingredients.
10. Repeat for other crust. Bake for 20 minutes.

Makes 2- 10" pizzas

+ SOY FREE +

Zulu Muffins

Ingredients

Dry

2 cups flour

2 tsp baking powder

1/4 tsp baking soda

2 tbsp flax seed meal

1 tsp allspice

Wet

3/4 cup non-GMO vegan margarine or coconut oil

2/3 cup sucanat

1/2 tsp pure vanilla extract

3/4 cup non-dairy milk

1 medium zucchini grated (1½ cup)

Directions:

Preheat oven to 350°.

1. Oil muffin pan or use muffin cups. Set aside.

2. In a large bowl, mix dry ingredients.

3. In a separate bowl, cream margarine and sucanat until well mixed.

4. Add remaining wet ingredients, mix well.

5. Add wet ingredients to dry then mix well.

6. Fill muffin pan with batter.

7. Bake at 350° for 20-25 minutes or until knife or toothpick poked in comes out clean.

Makes 12 muffins

+ SOY FREE. CAN BE MADE GLUTEN FREE IF GLUTEN FREE FLOUR IS USED. IF MAKING GLUTEN FREE, COOK FOR 10-15 MINUTE +

Nana Muffins

Ingredients

Dry

2 cups flour

2 tsp baking powder

2 tbsp flax seed meal

1 tsp cinnamon

½ cup nuts (optional)

Wet

3/4 cup margarine

1 cup agave, honey or maple syrup

1/2 tsp vanilla

½ cup vanilla almond milk

1 ¼ cup of very ripe, mashed bananas

Directions:

Preheat oven to 350°.

1. Use muffin cups or oil and flour a 12-muffin pan. Set aside.
2. In a large bowl sift and mix the dry ingredients.
3. In a separate bowl, cream margarine then add bananas and the remaining wet ingredients. Mix well.
4. Add wet ingredients to dry and mix well.
5. Pour batter into pan.
6. Bake for 20-25 minutes until toothpick poked in comes out clean.

Makes 12 muffins

+ SOY FREE. CAN BE MADE GLUTEN FREE IF GLUTEN FREE FLOUR IS USED. IF MAKING GLUTEN FREE, COOK FOR 10-15 MINUTE +

Basic Pie Crust

Ingredients

3 cups spelt flour

1 tsp of cinnamon

½ tsp sea salt

1/4 cup of agave

1 ½ cup of cold non GMO margarine or shortening cut into small pieces

¼ to ½ cup of iced water

Directions:

1. All ingredients, (except agave) should be icy cold and the flour should be frozen.
2. Add flour, cinnamon and salt to food processor. Pulse to combine.
3. Add the agave and margarine and pulse until mixture resembles coarse crumbs with some larger pieces remaining, about 10 seconds. To mix by hand, mix ingredients in a large bowl then cut with a pastry blender or fork.
4. With the machine running, add the ¼ cup of water through the feed tube in a slow and steady stream, just until the dough holds together without being wet or sticky. Do not process more than 30 seconds.
5. Test dough by squeezing a small amount of the dough together; if it's too crumbly, add a bit more water 1 tablespoon at a time.

Roll out dough and place in a pan.

6. Take the dough out and divide in half; shape into flattened rounds. Wrap with plastic and refrigerate for at least one hour or overnight.
7. Pre-bake oven to 350°.
8. Roll dough out and place into a pie pan. Poke with a fork around the bottom and pre bake for 5 minutes before you fill.

Trim the crust and use a fork to make a design around. Make a few holes by poking the bottom.

Makes 2 eight inch crusts

Serves 8-12

+ CAN BE MADE SOY FREE IF PALM SHORTENING IS USED +

Sweetie Pie

Ingredients

2 ½ cups of baked and mashed, red garnet sweet potatoes (about 3 medium)

2 tbsp flax seed meal

1/2 cup agave

1/4 cup 100% maple syrup

1 tsp cinnamon

1 tsp nutmeg

¼ tsp ginger

¼ cup of melted non-GMO margarine

¼ cup of flour

1/2 tbsp pure vanilla extract

2 pie crusts

Directions:

1. Bake unpeeled sweet potatoes in the oven at 450° for 50-55 minutes, turning once after 25 minutes.

2. Remove potatoes from oven and let cool enough to peel them.

3. Place an oven rack on 2nd to last shelf then preheat the oven to 350°.

4. Peel the potatoes then puree in food processor or mash in a large bowl.

5. Mix flax meal, agave, maple syrup, and potatoes in a bowl.

6. Heat cinnamon, nutmeg and ginger in a small skillet on medium/low heat for 30 sec. Then add the margarine to the pan and melt.

7. Add the mixture to the potatoes.

6. Add flour and vanilla and mix all ingredients with a hand mixer or food processor until smooth.

7. Pour mixture into a piecrust, leaving about ½" unfilled.

8. Cover top of pie crust with foil and place on bottom rack of the oven

9. Bake for 55-60 minutes.

10. Remove the foil during the last 10 minutes of baking.

Serves 8-10

Cut three strips of foil.

Fold the ends of each strip together.

Cover the top of the pie crust with foil.

The Original "Crown Heights" Apple Pie

Ingredients

5 medium golden delicious apples (8 cups)

3 tbsp of non-GMO margarine or coconut oil

1 tsp cinnamon

1 tsp nutmeg

1/2 tbsp vanilla extract

1/2 cup maple syrup

1/2 tbsp lemon juice

1/2 tbsp arrowroot powder (or cornstarch)

1 tbsp non-dairy milk

2 pie crusts

Directions:

Preheat oven to 350°.

1. Core and peel apples.
2. Cut apples into bite size pieces.
3. Simmer apples in pot for 5 minutes, covered.
4. Add remaining ingredients except for arrowroot and milk.
5. Simmer covered for 10 minutes.
6. In a small cup, mix arrowroot and milk.
7. Turn off apples, add arrowroot mixture, let stand for 5 minutes.
8. Pour mixture into piecrust, leaving about 1/8 cup liquid out. Cover pie with second crust alternating the strips.
9. Glaze top of crust with remaining liquid.
10. Put in oven on a cookie sheet.
11. Bake for 25-30 minutes. Cool completely before serving.

Using remaining dough cut strips for the top of the pie.

Alternate the strips making a weaving pattern and use a fork to seal the top to the bottom.

Serves 8-10

+ CAN BE MADE SOY FREE AND GLUTEN FREE IF COCONUT OIL IS USED AND A GLUTEN FREE CRUST +

Hood Rich Brownies

Ingredients

½ cup margarine or vegan shortening

½ cup sucanat

¼ cup maple syrup

1 ½ cups chocolate chips (divided)

¼ cup non-dairy milk

1 ½ tsp vanilla extract

Dry:

1 ¼ cup spelt or wheat flour

½ tsp baking soda

½ tsp salt

½ tsp baking powder (aluminum free)

2 tbsp flax seed meal

Directions:

1. Preheat the oven to 350°. Grease and flour a 9" square pan. Sit to the side. (see page 144)
2. Heat margarine, sucanat and maple syrup on a low heat until the margarine is melted.
3. Add 1 cup of chocolate chips and turn the heat off. Keep the pot on the burner and stir the mixture until the chips are melted.
4. Add the almond milk and vanilla. Sit to the side.
5. In a medium bowl, mix the dry ingredients.
6. Add the chocolate mixture to the dry ingredients and mix well. Add the remaining chips.
7. Spread the batter evenly into prepared pan.
8. Bake 25 minutes. Remove and let cool completely.
9. Cut into squares.

Serves 16

Carob Brownies Squares

Ingredients

¼ cup non-GMO margarine or oil

½ cup sucanat

¼ cup maple syrup

1½ cups carob chips (divided)

½ cup coconut milk

1½ tsp vanilla extract

Dry:

1¼ cup spelt or whole wheat flour

½ tsp baking soda

½ tsp salt

1 tsp baking powder

2 tbsp flax seed meal

Directions:

1. Preheat the oven to 350 degrees. Grease and flour a 9-inch square pan. Sit to the side.
2. Heat margarine, sucanat and maple syrup on a low heat until the margarine is melted.
3. Add 1 cup of carob chips and turn the heat off. Keep the pot on the burner and stir the mixture until the chips are melted.
4. Add the almond milk and vanilla. Sit to the side.
5. In a medium bowl, mix the dry ingredients.
6. Add the chocolate mixture to the dry ingredients and mix well. Add the remaining chips.
7. Spread the batter evenly into prepared pan.
8. Bake 20-25 minutes until toothpick stuck in the center comes out clean.
9. Remove and let cool completely.
10. Cut into squares.

Serves 16

Front: **SCRAMBLED TOFU** Pg 86

Back: **HEARTY BREAKFAST POTATOES** Pg 83

WACHE
BLACK EYED PEAS AND RICE

Pg 128

VEGETABLE FRIED RICE

Pg 127

SWEETIE PIE

Pg 139

SOUL FOOD MEAL
Top left going clockwise:

SWEETIE PIE, Pg 139, **COUNTRY CORN BREAD.** Pg 131. **BROWN PRIDE RICE.** Pg 125 **YAMS SWEET YAM.** Pg 120, **AL GREENS.** Pg 111, **PAN FRIED SEITAN.** Pg 152.

FRUIT KEBOBS

Pg 82

SESAME TOFU SALAD

Pg 94

Bottom going clockwise:

CHIMICHANGA, Pg 104, **GOOD OL' GUAC.** Pg 150, **BROOKLYN FRIED PLANTAINS.** Pg 123.

EAST INDIAN ROTI

Pg 133

MY MAMA'S POTATO SALAD

Pg 97

RICE NUT KRISPIES

Pg 144

STACKS
Pg 85

TEMPEH SAUXSAGE
Pg 87

VEGETABLE MISO SOUP

Pg 89

MASHEM UP'
Pg 121

HUSH PUPS

Pg 132

VEGAN GRILLIN'
Top left going counter clockwise:
VEGGIE HOT DOGS, VEGGIE FISH, VEGGIE BURGERS, PASTA-FARI SALAD page 96, **GRILLED TOFU-TATER WRAP** pg 106, **GRILLED TEMPEH KEBOBS, GOLD GRILLED CORN** pg 116, **MY MAMA'S POTATO SALAD** pg 97, **SWEET BAKED BEANS** pg 124.

GOLD GRILLED CORN

Pg 116

GO GREEN JUICE

Pg 149

CRISPY FRIED CAULIFLOWER

Pg 110

Top left going clockwise:
CINNAMON COCONUT COUS COUS, Pg 126, **CAN'T BELIEVE THIS IS SQUASH,** Pg 119. **DAAL,** Pg 108.

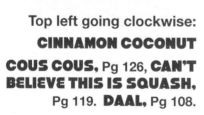

CRISPY COLLARD GREEN ROLLS

Pg 113

COMMUNITY COLESLAW

Pg 95

LEMON GRASS COCONUT SOUP

Pg 88

GARVEY SALAD

Pg 92

CAN'T BELIEVE ITS SQUASH

Pg 119

BUFFALO TOFU

Pg 102

HOOD RICH BROWNIES

Pg 141

MAC-N- CHEESE

Pg 130

NANA MUFFINS

Pg 137

Chocolate City Cookies

Ingredients
¾ cup non-hydrogenated margarine

1 cup sucanat

1 tsp vanilla extract

½ cup maple syrup

Dry:
2 ¼ cups spelt or whole wheat flour

1 tsp baking soda

1 tsp baking powder

2 tbsp flax seed meal

¼ tsp salt

2 cups vegan grain sweetened chips (chocolate or carob)

1 cup chopped walnuts or pecans

Directions:
1. Sit margarine out to soften.
2. In a large bowl, cream margarine by mixing with a spoon.
3. Add sucanat and mix well.
4. Add vanilla and maple syrup. Mix well.
5. In a separate bowl, mix the dry ingredients except the nuts and chips.
6. Combine all the ingredients and mix well.
7. Cover and refrigerate for at least 30 minutes.
8. Preheat oven to 350° and lightly grease a cookie sheet.
9. Spoon dough onto sheet a tablespoon at a time.
10. Bake for 8-10 minutes. (The bottoms should be golden brown)

For bars, add mix to a 13" x 9" oiled and floured pan and bake for 25- 30 minutes.

Serves 16

Rice Nut Krispies

Ingredients
4 cups of brown rice krisp cereal

½ cup of peanut butter

½ cup of agave or honey

Directions:
1. Lightly oil a 9½" x13" inch pan.
2. In a large pot, add peanut butter and agave and melt on a medium/low heat.
3. Turn heat off, add cereal and mix well.
4. Spoon mixture into the pan or smaller one if you want thicker bars.
5. Press mix evenly in the pan with a spoon or your hands.
6. Let cool and refrigerate for at least 30 minutes. Cut into squares.

Serves 12-16

+ SOY AND GLUTEN FREE +

....

Flouring A Pan
1. Pour 1 tbsp of oil in the pan. Fully coat the pan using a napkin or paper towel.
2. Add 1-2 tbsp of flour to the pan. Shake and tap the pan to cover it with flour.
3. Floured pan.

Karamu Corn

This is a rendition of the classic caramel corn

Ingredients

1 cup sucanat

½ cup maple syrup

1 tbsp molasses

½ cup almond milk

¼ tsp sea salt

2 tbsp margarine

9 cups of popped popcorn (2/3 cup kernels)

1 cup of roasted peanuts

1 tsp baking soda

Directions:

1. In a medium pot add all ingredients except baking soda, popcorn and peanuts.
2. On a medium/low heat, bring the mix to a simmer for 30 minutes, stirring occasionally. If the mixture bubbles up to the top of the pan, turn the heat down slightly.
3. Preheat oven to 250 degrees.
4. Add popcorn and peanuts to a large pan or cookie sheet.
5. Turn the caramel sauce off and add the baking soda. The sauce will turn foamy.
6. Pour the caramel mixture over the popcorn and peanuts and mix well making sure the popcorn is covered as much as possible.
7. Place pan in the oven and bake for 5 minutes. Stir popcorn mixture every three minutes making sure all pieces are covered.
8. Take the pan out and immediately put the popcorn into the container you plan to store it in or it will stick to the pan.
9. Let cool completely and enjoy!

Serves 5

+ GLUTEN FREE +

BEVERAGES

Spirulina Shake

Ingredients

1½ cups frozen bananas

1½ cups vanilla non-dairy ice cream

1 tsp of Spirulina

1 cup of non-dairy milk

Directions:

1. Add all ingredients to the blender.

2. Blend until smooth. Add more milk if necessary.

Serves 2 people

+ SOY AND GLUTEN FREE +

....

Peach Cobbler Smoothie

Ingredients

¼ cup of frozen mangos

¼ cup of frozen peaches

1 tsp grated ginger

3 cubes or 3 tbsp sea moss (frozen or fresh)- optional

1 dash of cinnamon

1 tbsp agave

¼ cup of coconut milk

1 cup of apple juice

Directions:

1. Add all ingredients to the blender except the juice and mix.

2. Add apple juice and blend until smooth.

Makes 2 Servings

+ SOY AND GLUTEN FREE +

✳ VSG: SMOOTHIE GUIDE

Many times people feel like they cannot make a smoothie with out a recipe but they are really just a combination of your favorite fruit, milk and juice. Below is a guide on the types of ingredients used as a basic recipe.

½ to 1 cup of fruit (fresh or frozen)
1/2 to 1 cup frozen bananas
1 to 2 cups of liquid
1 to 2 tsp of natural sweetener
1tsp- 2 tbsp of supplement (optional)

If the smoothie is not mixing well or if you like your smoothie more watery add ¼ cup of water at a time as needed.

Liquid Base

You can choose which one you like depending on the type of smoothie you're making. Milk and yogurt bases go better with nut butters and nut butter's go great with just about any fruit. Juices go better with fruit and berries. Mixing milk, kefir and yogurt are also helpful if you are not a fan of yogurt and kefir but want the benefits of them.

Non-dairy milk   Non-dairy yogurt
Non-dairy kefir   100% citrus fruit juice (orange, pineapple, mango)

Fruit Base

Frozen -Bananas, Pineapples, berries, mangos, peaches, cherries and mixed fruit mixes
Fresh -Cantaloupe, mango, peaches, oranges and berries

Nut Butters

Peanut butter, raw or roasted almond butter, tahini and cashew butter

Supplement

Supplements can give an added boost of nutrients for weight gain, weight loss or just get more nutrients in your kids. Spirulina and chlorella will make a smoothie green so they work best with yellow or orange color fruits. If they are mixed with berries they will give the smoothie a brown muddy color. Aloe has a strong taste so 1-2 tsp at the most is good.

Seamoss, spirulina, chlorella, aloe, ¼ inch ginger, ¼ of an avocado and protein powder

Green Goddess Smoothie

Ingredients

1 cup of frozen bananas

3 cubes or 3 tbsp sea moss (frozen or fresh)- optional

1 cup of fresh cantaloupe

1 tsp of Spirulina

1 tbsp of flax seed oil

1 cup of apple juice (divided)

Directions:

1. Add all ingredients and ½ cup of apple juice to the blender.
2. Blend fruit, add remaining juice then blend until smooth.

Makes 2 Servings

+ SOY AND GLUTEN FREE +

Hemp My Smoothie

Ingredients

¼ cup hemp seeds***

2 frozen bananas

1 cup almond milk (divided)

1 tsp agave

Directions:

1. Add all ingredients and ½ cup of almond milk to the blender then blend.
2. Add remaining milk then blend until smooth.
3. Add more milk ½ cup at a time if you'd like it more watery.

***Tip: If you have a grinder, grind the seeds before you add them.

Makes 2 Servings

+ SOY AND GLUTEN FREE +

Go Green Juice

Ingredients

1 large cucumber

4 sweet apples (red or green)

4 collard green or kale leaves

1 lemon without the peel

1 inch of fresh ginger (optional)

8 oz of water

Directions:

1. Using your juicer, juice 2 apples, collard greens, and lemon first then add remaining apples, ginger and the cucumber.
2. Run the water through the juicer to add to the juice.
3. Using another cup, mix juice (including foam) back and forth in between both cups until mixed.
4. Refrigerate and drink within 4 hours or freeze.

Party of 3

+ SOY AND GLUTEN FREE +

Green Light Cocktail

Ingredients

2 cubes of frozen wheat grass (or 2 oz of fresh)*

8 oz apple cider or dark apple juice

The juice of ½ lemon

Directions:

1. Add all ingredients to a glass and stir.
2. The cocktail is ready when all the ice has melted.

*if you use fresh wheat grass add 2 ice cubes

Makes 1 Serving

+ SOY AND GLUTEN FREE +

SAUCES AND DIPS

Good ol' Guac

Ingredients

¼ cup minced onions

½ cup chopped tomatoes

2 avocadoes, chopped

1 tbsp fresh, chopped cilantro

¼ tsp sea salt

Juice of ½ lime

Pinch of cayenne

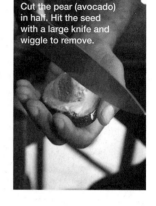

Cut the pear (avocado) in half. Hit the seed with a large knife and wiggle to remove.

Directions:

Add all ingredients to a bowl and mix using a potato masher or fork.

Serves a Party of 4

+ SOY AND GLUTEN FREE +

Motza Cheez Sauce

Ingredients

¼ cup milk

½ cup oil

1 ½ tbsp lemon juice

1 tsp Dijon mustard

½ cup soft tofu

¼ cup nutritional yeast

1/4 tsp sea salt

2 tsp granulated garlic

1 tbsp soy sauce

1 tsp agave

Directions:

1. Add all ingredients to a blender and blend until smooth.
2. The sauce does not have much of a taste when it's first made but as it cooks it is wonderful!

Makes 1 ½ -2 cups

+ CAN BE MADE GLUTEN FREE IF WHEAT FREE SOY SAUCE IS USED +

Mushroom Gravy

Ingredients

2 tbsp oil

1 tbsp flour

½ cup dried mushroom + 1 cup hot water

1 tbsp soy sauce

1 tbsp nutritional yeast

¾ cup veggie broth

Veggies

¼ cup green peppers, diced

¼ cup onions, diced

2 cloves garlic, diced

Spices:

1 tsp of each: parsley, granulated garlic, ground ginger, ground mustard seed

½ tsp thyme or rosemary

½ tsp black pepper

Directions:

1. Pour water over mushrooms and let sit.
2. Add flour and oil to a small pot and sauté on a medium/low heat until golden brown, about 3-4 minutes.
3. Add the veggies and sauté 5 min on medium/low heat.
4. Add spices and sauté for 30 sec.
5. Add the remaining ingredients including the mushrooms with water.
6. Simmer on low for 20 minutes, stirring occasionally.
7. The gravy can be strained through a colander or kept chunky.

Serves 4-6

COOKING WITH TOFU

Marinated

Marinating tofu gives it flavor. It can be enhanced and used in many cuisines. Marinate with curry, thai, Indian or soulfood seasonings.

Broiled

My friends Fire and Yvette introduced me to broiling tofu. It's simple and takes very little effort. Preheat broiler. Arrange marinated tofu in 1 layer in baking pan. Adding a small amount of oil to the bottom of the pan is optional. Pour remaining marinade over tofu. Broil 4 to 6 inches from heat until golden brown, about 10 minutes. Turn and cook the other side. The second side may take less time (about 8 minutes). Periodically check both sides while cooking to prevent burning. Frozen or regular tofu can be used.

Pan-fried

Heat a pan on a medium heat. Then fill it with oil up to 1-inch. Add marinated tofu.   Lightly brown the tofu on both sides about 5 minutes each side. After its fried add any of your favorite sauces: BBQ, jerk, curry or terryaki.

Deep-fried

Heat a pan on a medium/high heat. Then fill it one-third or halfway up with oil. Dredge each piece of tofu in arrowroot (or cornstarch), flour, cornmeal or a wet batter. Drop the tofu into oil and cook about 5 minutes, frying the pieces until golden brown and crispy. Remove and drain on a rack or paper towel.

Grilled

Lay foil on top of the grill and poke holes in it so the tofu can get some of the grill flavoring. Brush the tofu with oil to help it from sticking. Cook on both sides until brown.

Baked

Marinate the tofu. Preheat the oven to 400 degrees. Pour half of the remaining marinade along with 1 tbsp of oil into a 9x15 pan. Lay tofu in an even layer. Pour the remaining marinade over tofu. Bake for 30 minutes uncovered, turning after 15 minutes. If you are using gravy or a sauce, bake tofu without gravy for 15 minutes, uncovered. Flip the tofu then pour on remaining gravy/sauce. Cover with foil and bake 15 more minutes.

CUTTING TOFU

Below are 5 different ways to cut tofu:

Sliced

Steaks

Strips

Nuggets

Cubes

COOKING WITH WHOLE GRAINS

Grains are carbohydrates that serve as energy in your body. There are many types of whole grains and rice to choose from.

Grains have only been in the human diet for 12,000 years. They contain a natural pesticide called phytic acid that stops insects from eating them. Phytic acids may have health effects on humans by carrying necessary nutrients like calcium out of the body. Phytic acid can be removed by soaking and washing the grains. Grains can also be sprouted to increase their enzymes and digestibility. People who have gluten (the protein in flour) and grain sensitivities can sometimes tolerate spouted grains as well as flours and breads made from them.

Grains	Water	Grain amount	Cooking Time
Barley	3 cup	1 cup	45min
Buck wheat	2 cup	1 cup	15 min
Bulgur	2 cup	1 cup	15 min
Grits (yellow corn)*	4 cup	1 cup	10-12 min
Millet*	2.5 cup	1 cup	20 min
Oats			
Rolled	3 cup	1 cup	10 min
Quick	2 cup	1 cup	5 min
Quinoa*	2 cup	1 cup	20 min
Rice*			
Brown basmati	2 cup	1 cup	35-40 min
Brown long grain	2 cup	1 cup	45 min
Brown short grain	2 cup	1 cup	45 min
Wild	3 cup	1 cup	60 min
Pasta			
Couscous	4 cups	1 cup	5 min
*Corn	5 quarts (24 cups)	1 package	8-9 min
*Quinoa	3 quarts (14 cups)	1 package	4-6 min
*Rice	5 quarts	1 package	2-9 min
Spelt	3 quarts	1 package	3-7 min
Whole wheat	3 quarts	1 package	10 min

*Gluten free

Cooking whole grain pastas:

Whole grain pastas cook much quicker than refined/white pastas. They can also become mushy quickly so after cooking, strain and immediately run cold water over the pasta to stop it from cooking.

COOKING WITH BEANS

Beans can be healing as well as nourishing. They contain calcium, iron and B vitamins. When they are sprouted (bean sprouts), they are great sources of Vitamin C and enzymes.

What About The Gas?

Some people suffer from gas and poor digestibility when they eat beans.
A few options to reduce the gassiness of beans are:
-Soaking the beans overnight and strainsoaking water frequently
-Removing bubbles with a spoon that form at the top of the pot when the beans are cooking.
- Add kombu (seaweed) to beans while they are cooking
- Add fennel while cooking or eat a few seeds after your meal

**Young children under the age of 18 months have difficulty digesting harder beans/peas. Green beans and green peas are best.

Bean prep:

For dry beans there are a few options:
1. Wash and soak the beans over night or for 6-8 hours making sure the beans are fully covered with water.
Or,
2. The hot soak method: Wash beans then place them in a pot and cover with 3-4" of water. Bring to a boil and cook for 5 min. Remove the pot from heat. Cover and let beans soak in the water for 2 hours. Strain then cook.

** Salt can toughen beans so add near the end of cooking. If you'd like to keep the skins together, add salt in the first third of cooking time (beans that cook for 60 min- add salt after 20 min)

Beans (legumes)	Liquid/ 1 cup of dry beans	Liquid/ 1 cup of frozen beans	Cooking time Dry/frozen (min)	Digestibility
Adzuki/Aduki	3 ¼	3	45 /30	easy
Black	4	3	75 /45	hard
Black eyed Peas	4	3	75 / 35	moderate
Chickpeas (Garbanzo)	4	3	3-4 hrs/60	hard
Great Northern	4	3	90 /45	moderate
Kidney	4	3	2 hrs/20	hard
Red Lentils	2	-	20	easy
French (brown)Lentils	3	-	45	easy
Lima	3	3	60-90/	easy
Navy	4	3	60/ 35	hard
Pinto	4	3	60/ 45	hard
Split Peas	3	-	60-90	easy
Mung beans	4	-	60	easy

TOOLS YOU NEED

Here are a few tools you should have handy to make the recipes in the book

Spice Grinder & Air Popper
Food Processor
Blender
Juicer

The Basics- A pot set, spoon/spatulas, pan set, a cast iron skillet and a medium and large non-stick frying pan.

Tongs- To flip tofu or fried foods.

Tongs & Knives

Spice grinder- To grind seeds or spices.

Blender- Used for smoothies and sauces.

Juicer- is used for making fresh fruit and vegetable juices. Juicers can range from $60-$1200. I have had a $1200 one and a $150 one. The $1200 juicer was more of an industrial juicer that was good for high volume juicing like for a restaurant. The $150 juicer was more of a juicer for the home and worked very well. My mother has a Juice Man Jr and that works pretty well. You are supposed to buy a juicer based on how much juice you get from the fruit or vegetable, but I have yet to be able to find that out. If you buy a juicer make sure you buy it from somewhere you can return it if you don't like it. Some juicers have to stay in one spot or else they will start to vibrate uncontrollably. If that's the kind you have, take it back and try another brand.

Air popcorn popper- An inexpensive way to save you from eating microwave popcorn, which can have high amounts of hydrogenated oils and salt.

Food processor- A food processor can be helpful in making pie dough and for quick chopping.

MENU PLANNING

Some Tips:

Don't let any fruit go bad; freeze it for smoothies.

Freeze leftovers for lunch.

Freeze fresh juices and smoothies to have during the week.

Add vegetables to as many meals and snacks as you can.

Day 1 Breakfast- scrambled tofu with Minute spinach and herbal tea

Lunch- Lemongrass coconut soup, kale salad and water

Dinner- Southern Fried Tofu, Yams Sweet Yams, Al Greens

Snacks- non-dairy ice cream, fruit, water

Day 2 Breakfast- fruit smoothie

Lunch- Sesame Tofu Salad, water

Dinner- Down Home chili, blue corn chips, Brooklyn Fried plantains

Juice or herbal tea

Snacks- fruit, water, popcorn

Day 3 Breakfast- Sunday grits, soy bacon or sausage, whole grain pancakes, 100 % maple syrup.

Lunch- Savory Brazil sauxsage with lettuce and a smoothie

Dinner- Pepper Steak, Brown Pride rice and salad

Juice or herbal tea

Snacks- water, fruit, chips

Day 4 Breakfast- oatmeal, herbal tea or water

Lunch- lentil soup, peanut butter and jelly on whole grain bread

Dinner- Tofu tater wrap with Pasta-fari salad

Snacks- water, fruit, whole grain graham crackers

Day 5 Breakfast- whole grain cereal with non-dairy milk

Lunch- bean burrito, water

Dinner- salad with sautéed tofu or canned lentils, shredded carrots, tomatoes with Italian, French, honey mustard, or non- dairy salad dressing.

Veggie pizza

Juice or herbal tea

Snacks- fruit, water, whole grain pretzels with hummus

Day 6 Breakfast- fruit salad, water or herbal tea

Lunch- taco salad with red beans, brown rice, lettuce, soy cheese, tomatoes, salsa, olives, onions, and blue corn chips, water

Dinner- Daal, coconut cous cous and salad

Snacks- fruit, nuts, trail mix, cereal with non-dairy milk, water

Day 7   Breakfast- scrambled tofu with veggies, yellow corn grits
Lunch- Miso soup, Garvey salad, juice
Dinner- Creole red beans, Brown Pride rice, coconut collard greens, corn on the cob
Water or herbal iced tea
Snacks- hood rich brownies, fruit, blue corn chips and salsa

SHOPPING LIST

Many times I have been asked, "If you don't eat meat, milk or dairy, than what do you eat?" I humbly have to say that there is a wide array of other foods to eat. Below I have listed my basic shopping list and things I like to keep on hand. Fruits and vegetables will be available based on the season.

Vegetables

Asparagus
Artichoke
Broccoli
Brussel sprouts
Cauliflower
Carrots
Celery
Corn
Cucumber
Greens (collards, kale, chard)
Green beans
Green peas
Green bell pepper
Garlic
Ginger root
Lettuce (green leaf or romaine)
Mushrooms
Onions
Potatoes
Plantains
Squash (winter or summer)
Spinach
Tomatoes
Yams (sweet potatoes)

Fruits

Apples
Avocadoes
Blueberries
Bananas
Cherries
Cantaloupe
Dates
Figs
Grapes
Grapefruits
Honeydew melon
Kiwi
Lemons
Limes
Mangoes
Oranges
Pears
Peaches
Plums
Pineapples
Strawberries
Watermelon

Dry/canned goods

Grains:
Brown rice
Couscous
Cereal
Corn tortillas
Cornmeal
Flour (spelt or whole wheat)
Grits (yellow corn)
Oatmeal
Pasta (whole grain, gluten free)
Whole grain bread

Beans

Canned or dry beans:
chickpeas, brown lentils, black beans, red beans, lima beans, red lentils, black-eyed peas, adzuki bean and white beans.

Nuts/Seeds

Flax seeds/ meal
Hemp seeds
Almonds
Walnuts or pecans
Peanuts

Snacks

Raisins
Applesauce
Fruit bars
Potato chips
Corn chips
Popcorn
Corn thins
Cookies
Rice cakes
Nut butters (peanut, almond, cashew and sunflower)
Jelly or Preserves

Beverages

Non Dairy milk (almond, soy, rice, coconut or oat)
Kefir
100% Fruit juice
Herbal tea (peppermint, chamomile, kombucha, yerba mate)

Condiments

Soy sauce
Bragg's liquid amino acids
Ketchup
Mustard
Bbq sauce
Nutritional yeast

Misc

Kombu (kelp)
Vegetable broth
Cream of mushroom soup (broth)
Coconut milk
Oil (olive, sesame, peanut, coconut, toasted sesame, hemp)
White Palm oil
Agave or honey
Maple syrup
Sucanat
Baking powder (aluminum-free)
Baking soda
Arrowroot (or corn starch)

Spices

This seems like a lot of spices, but these are basic seasonings that can be added to many dishes.

Black pepper
Cinnamon
Chili powder
Cilantro
Cayenne pepper
Ginger (ground)
Garlic (granulated/powder)
Italian seasoning
Mustard seed (ground)
Mushrooms (dried)
Nutmeg
Onion (granulated/powder)
Oregano
Parsley
Sea salt
Sage
Thyme

Refrigerator:

Cream cheese (tofu)
Fruit juice100%
Hummus
Margarine (veggie and non-Gmo)
Olives
Pickles
Salsa
Tofu (soft and extra firm)
Tempeh
Veggie bacon
Whole grain/corn tortilla
Non dairy yogurt

Frozen:

Beans
Edammame
Fruit
French fries
Ice cream (non-dairy)

Pizza crust
Pie crust
Vegetables
Waffles

Supplements
Chlorella
Flax seed oil
Hemp oil
Spirulina

✳ SUBSTITUTION BASICS

Non Vegan	Vegan
Bacon	Tempeh bacon, veggie bacon
Hamburger	Tvp granules, veggie burger, ground seitan
Chicken	Tofu, tvp steaks or chunks
Chicken or beef broth	Vegetable broth, vegetable bullion cubes
1 egg	1tbp of flax seed meal mixed with 3 tbsp non dairy milk ¼ cup silken/soft tofu
1 cup cow's milk	1 cup of fortified non dairy milk (almond, oat, soy, coconut or rice milk
1 cup yogurt	1 cup soy yogurt (soy or coconut)
Mayonnaise	Garvey salad dressing blended with 1 cup of soft tofu (see page 92), Non dairy mayonnaise,
Cheese	Motza cheese (see page 150), non dairy cheese (soy, rice), nutritional yeast, tofu cream cheese and tofu sour cream
Ricotta cheese	Soft tofu mashed and mixed with lemon and nutritional yeast Soft tofu mashed mixed with tofu cream cheese
Ice cream	Non dairy ice cream (Soy, rice, almond and coconut), vegan sherbet or sorbet and popsicles
Butter	Non dairy margarine, olive oil and coconut oil
1 cup sugar	1 cup sucanat ½ cup agave mixed with ½ cup maple syrup (decrease the amount of liquid by ½-3/4 cup)
1 cup brown sugar	¾ cup of sucanat mixed with ¼ cup maple syrup 1 cup maple syrup (decrease the amount of liquid by ½-3/4 cup)

tsp= teaspoon
tbsp= tablespoon
g= gram
mg= milligram
8 ounces (oz) = 1 cup
16 ounces (oz) = 1 pound
lb = pound

GLOSSARY

AL DENTE (al-den-tay)
In cooking, al dente describes pasta, rice or beans that have been cooked so as to be firm but not hard or too soft. It allows for the pasta to be baked or cooked again in another liquid without getting mushy.

DDT - Dichlorodiphenyltrichloroethane
DDT was developed as an insecticide in the 1940s, and was widely used during World War II to combat insect-borne diseases. DDT's effectiveness, persistence, and low cost made it popular for uses such as insecticides and pesticides in farming and in the home. More than a billion pounds were used in the U.S. over a 30-year period. EPA banned nearly all domestic uses of DDT in 1972 and over 160 countries have also banned the use unless extremely necessary. Today, use of DDT is limited to malaria control programs in some developing countries. Human exposure to DDT has been linked to n increase risk of infant mortality as well as breast, liver and pancreatic cancer. Even though DDT is banned in the US we are still exposed to it through our drinking water and foods from other countries.

Expeller Pressed
A method where oil is squeezed from the seed, nut or fruit, under high pressure without heating or chemical extraction.

DIOXINS
According to the National Institute of Environmental Health Services, Dioxins are a class of chemical contaminants that are formed during processes such as waste incineration, forest fires, backyard trash burning, paper pulp bleaching and herbicide manufacturing. The highest environmental concentrations of dioxin are usually found in soil, air and water. Humans are primarily exposed to dioxins by eating food contaminated by these chemicals such as beef, pork, chicken, dairy products and vegetables. Dioxin accumulates in the fat tissues in the body, where they may stay for months or years. Exposure to high levels of dioxins can cause an increased risk of heart disease, diabetes, cancer as well as reproductive and developmental problems.

FLAXSEED MEAL
Flax seed meal is a powdered form of ground up flax seeds. It's high in fiber and omega 3 fatty acids. Flax seed meal can be used as a substitute for eggs in baking.

KEFIR
Kefir is made from gelatinous white or yellow particles called "grains" that are made of beneficial yeast as well as friendly 'probiotic' bacteria. The grains are added to milk (soy or coconut as well) and are made in to an acidic yogurt like drink. Kefir is considered to be beneficial to the digestive and immune systems.

MISO

Miso is a fermented bean paste (usually made from soy). In addition to soybeans, some miso also feature chickpeas, rice, barley, or wheat. Miso ranges in color from white, brown and red. The lighter varieties are less salty and more mellow in flavor while the darker ones are saltier and have a more intense flavor.

PCBs (Polychlorinated Biphenyl)

PCBs belong to a broad family of man-madenchemicals known as chlorinated hydrocarbons. PCBs were manufactured in the US from 1929 until their production was banned in 1979. PCBs were used in hundreds of industrial and commercial applications including as plasticizers in paints, plastics, and rubber products; in pigments, dyes, and carbonless copy paper; and many other industrial applications. Even though there production was banned in the US traces of the chemical is still found in water and soil today. PCBs have been demonstrated to cause cancer, as well as a variety of other adverse health effects on the immune system, reproductive system, nervous system, and endocrine system.

PROCESSED FOODS

Processed foods have been altered from their natural state for reasons of convenience or to kill bacteria. The methods used for processing foods include canning, freezing, refrigeration, dehydration and sterilization. Processed foods can be helpful such as canned or frozen foods allow for quick use or the ability to have certain fruits and vegetable all year long. They can also be harmful such as soda, candy, cookies, cereal and white bread that may be full of sugar, artificial ingredients, preservatives and colors that could lead to chronic disease such as diabetes and obesity.

PHYTATES

Phytates (phytic acid) are a type of salt that is found in grains, bran, beans, dried legumes and some nuts. Phytates can bind to calcium, iron, and zinc and make them unavailable for absorption in the body. Soaking and fermenting these food products help to reduce their phytate content.

WHOLE FOODS

Whole foods are basically foods that have not been changed or have been minimally changed from when they were picked or harvested. They are unprocessed and unrefined, or processed and refined as little as possible before being consumed and typically do not contain added ingredients, such as sugar, salt, or fat. For example brown rice is a whole food but pasta made from brown rice isn't. The term is often confused with organic food but all whole foods are not necessarily organic, nor are organic foods necessarily whole, although they do share a number of traits. So a non organic apple is a whole food but it have been grown using pesticides and herbicides. Examples of whole foods are: Fresh fruits and vegetables and brown rice

Illustrations by goldi gold

RESOURCES

RESOURCES

Dr. Afrika

African Holistic Health Group

P.O. Box 1645

Grand Rapids, MI 49501

For telephone consultations please call 317-216-8088.

For additional information please call (616) 446-2133.

For ordering questions please call (616) 828-5301.

www.drafrika.com

Queen Afua

HEAL THYSELF CENTRE

106 Kingston Ave.

Brooklyn, NY 11213

Phone: 718-221-HEAL

E-mail: info@queenafuaonline.com

www.queenafuaonline.com/hba/pages/home.htm

/www.queenafuaonline.com/sacredacademycertification.htm

The Black Vegetarian Society

Georgia (www.bvsga.org)

New York (www.bvsny.org)

Texas (www.bvstx.org)

Truly Living Well Natural Urban Farms

P.O. Box 90841

East Point, GA 30364

www.trulylivingwell.com

May Wah Healthy Vegetarian Food Inc.

213 Hester Street,

New York, NY 10013

Tele: 212.334.4428

Fax: 212.334.4423

www.vegieworld.com

*for veggie meat

Soul Vegetarian™ - Restaurants

www.kingdomofyah.com

Source of Life Juice Bar & Deli
(Inside Everlasting Life Health Food Store)
Soul Vegetarian Gourmet - Hampton Mall
9185 Central Avenue - Largo, MD 20743
(301) 324-6900

Soul Vegetarian Restaurant & Exodus Carry-Out
2606 Georgia Ave. NW - Washington, DC 20001
(202) EAT-SOUL (328-7685)

Source of Life Juice Bar & Deli
(Inside Everlasting Life Health Food Store)
2928 Georgia Avenue NW - Washington, DC 20010
(202) 232-1700

Soul Vegetarian East
205 E. 75th St. - Chicago, IL 60619
(773) 224-0104

Soul Vegetarian Restaurant
879-A Ralph Abernathy Blvd. SW - Atlanta, GA 30310
(404) 752-5194

Soul Vegetarian International
652 North Highland - Atlanta, GA 30306
(404) 874-0145

Eternity Vegetarian Deli & Juice Bar
11 South Euclid Ave., St. Louis, MO 63108
(314) 454-1851

Soul Vegetarian South
3225-A Rivers Avenue North - Charleston, SC 29405
(843) 744-1155

Israel

Taim Hakaim (Taste of Life) I
60 Ben Yehuda St. - Tel Aviv, Israel
011-972-3-620-3151

Taim Hakaim (Taste of Life) II
1433/1 Sederot Aliyah - Dimona, Israel 86000

Ghana, West Africa

Assase Pa (The Earth is Good)
AMA Compound - High Street
Accra, Ghana, West Africa
021-761936

Assase Pa Health & Wellness Resort
Cape Coast, Ghana, West Africa
042-309132
Carribean

Soul Vegetarian Complex
One DA Diamond - Sunny Isle
Christiansted, St. Croix, U.S.V.I. 00822
(340) 778-4080

GENERAL REFERENCES

Brooks (1975), *Peanuts and Colonialism: Consequences of the commercialisation of peanuts in West Africa, 1830-1870,* in "Journal of African History, vol. 16, no. 1, pp. 29-54. http://www.afrol.com/archive/groundnuts_gambia.htm

Carney (1986), *The social history of Gambian rice production: an analysis of food security strategies,* PhD thesis, Michigan State University, Ann Arbour.

Fyhri (1998), *The Gambia: The complexity of modernising the agricultural Sector in Africa, thesis in geography,* University of Oslo.

Weil (1984), *Slavery, groundnuts, and European capitalism in the Wuli kingdom of Senegambia, 1820-1930,* in "Research in Economic Anthropology," vol. 6, pp. 77-119.

Afrika L. *Nutricide: The nutritional destruction of the black race.* Brooklyn, NY. A&B; 2000.

Newhouse S. *Complete Natural Food Facts.* Thorsons; 1991-05-09

Balch JF, Balch PA. *Prescription for Dietary Wellness, Using Foods to Heal.* Garden City Park, NY. Avery; 1992-98

Health Benefits
Mangels A, Melina V, Messina V. Position of the American Dietetic Association and Dieticians of Canada: Vegetarian Diets. *Journal of the American Dietetic Association.* June 2003; vol 103(6), 748-765-

Meat
Ecoli/food poisoning
Food Safety Inspection Service. Food Safety Education. Available at: http://www.fsis.usda.gov/Food_Safety_Education/index.asp. Accessed October 15, 2009.

Chao A, Thun MJ, Connell CJ, et al. Meat consumption and the risk of colorectal cancer. *Journal of the American Medical Association.* January 2005; 293(2).

Chicken
Burros M. Chicken with arsenic? *Is that O.K?* New York Times [online]. April 5, 2006; Available at: http://www.nytimes.com/2006/04/05/dining/05well.html. Accessed October 16, 2009.

Nestle M. *What to Eat.* Union Square West, NY: North Point Press; 2006. 163

Fish
Mozaffarian D. Fish Intake, Contaminants, and Human Health: Evaluating the Risks and Benefits. *Journal of the American Medical Association.* 2006;296(15): 1885-1899

Pigs
Food and Drug Administration. Freedom of Information Summary, Supplemental New Animal Drug Application [online docket]. Available at: http://www.fda.gov/ohrms/dockets/98fr/140-863-fois001.pdf. Accessed October 17, 2009.

Dairy
www.whymilk.com

Vegan Nutrients
United States Department of Agriculture. Nutrient Data Laboratory. Food and Nutrition Information Center webpage. 2008. Available at: http://www.riley.nal.usda.gov/index.html. Accessed October 17, 2009.

Ostlund RE Jr. Phytosterols in human nutrition. *Annu Rev Nutr.* [serial online]. 2002; 22: 533-49. Available from: PubMed. Accessed October 17, 2009.

DHA/EPA Omega-3 Institute. Overview of Omega-3 Fatty Acids webpage. 2008. Available at: http://dhaomega3.org/index.php?category=overview. Accessed October 17, 2009.

United States Department of Agriculture. Nutrition Table by Food, Soy Stache. USDA Nutrient Database. 2008. Available at: http://www.soystache.com/foodtable.htm. Accessed October 17, 2009.

Pitchford P. *Healing with Whole Foods: Asian traditions and modern nutrition.* 3rd Ed. Berkeley, CA: North Atlantic; 2002.

Nutrition Data Know what you eat. Nutrition Facts. 2008. Available at: www.nutritiondata.com/facts-C-00001c20ic.html. Accessed October 17, 2009.

New York State Department of Health. Vitamin D and Healthy Bones. 2004. Available at: http://www.health.state.ny.us/diseases/conditions/osteoporosis/vitd.htm. Accessed October 17, 2009.

Oils and Fats

Environmental Protection Agency. Hexane Hazard Summary. Technology Transfer Network Air Toxics Web Site. Available at: http://www.epa.gov/ttn/atw/hlthef/hexane.html. 2000. Accessed October 17, 2009.

Environmental Protection Agency. N-Hexane. Integrated Risk Information System. 2005. Available at: http://www.epa.gov/iris/subst/0486.htm. Accessed October 17, 2009.

Saturated Fats

Guthrie J, Lin BH. Nutrition Quality of American Children's Diets. USDA publication webpage. 2000. Available at: http://www.ers.usda.gov/publications/foodreview/jan1996/frjan96c.pdf. Accessed October 17, 2009.

Organic Food

Food and Agricultural Organization of the United Nations. Organic Agriculture. 2008. Available at: http://www.fao.org/organicag/faq.jsp. Accessed October 17, 2009.

Human Genome Project Information. Genetically Modified Foods and Organisms. 2007. Available at: http://www.ornl.gov/sci/techresources/Human_Genome/elsi/gmfood.shtml. Accessed October 17, 2009.

The World Health Organization. 20 Questions on genetically Modified Foods. 2008. Available at: http://www.who.int/foodsafety/publications/biotech/20questions/en/index.html. Accessed October 17, 2009.

Biosolids

Environmental Protection Agency. Use and Disposal of Biosolids. 2003. Available at: http://www.epa.gov/waterscience/biosolids. Accessed October 17, 2009.

Center for Food Safety. Food Irradiation. 2008. http://www.centerforfoodsafety.org/index.cfm.

Accessed October 17, 2009.

Center for Disease Control. Food Irradiation: Division of Bacterial and Mycotic Diseases. 2005. http://www.cdc.gov/ncidod/dbmd/diseaseinfo/foodirradiation.htm#howaffect. Accessed October 17, 2009.

The Canadian Coalition for Nuclear Responsibility. Potential Health Hazards of Food Irradiation. 1987. Available at: http://www.ccnr.org/food_irradiation.html. Accessed October 17. 2009.

Tritsch GL. Food Irradiation. Roswell Park Cancer Institute. 2000. Available at: http://www.fda. gov/ohrms/dockets/dailys/00/Nov00/111300/c005218.pdf. Accessed October 17, 2009.

Pesticides/ Herbicide
Environmental Protection Agency. Human Health Issues. Pesticides Health and Safety. 2008. Available at: http://www. Epa.gov/pesticides/health/human.html. Accessed October 17, 2009.

Foods to avoid
Food and Drug Administration. Microwave Oven Radiation web page. CDRH Consumer Information. 2008. Available at: http://www.fda.gov/RadiationEmittingProducts/ResourcesforYouRadiationEmittingProducts/Consumers/ucm142616.htm. Accessed October 17, 2009.

Meadows M. Plastics and the Microwave. FDA Consumer Magazine website. 2002. Available at: http://fda.gov/fdac/features/2002/602_plastic.html. Accessed October 17, 2009.

Effect of coffee drinking on platelets: inhibition of aggregation and phenols incorporation.The British Journal of Nutrition [0007-1145] Natella . 2008,100 (6). 1276 -1282

Food and Drug Administration. Microwave Ovens. FDA Radiological Health Program website. 2007. Available at: http://www.fda.gov/cdrh/radhealth/products/microwave/html. Accessed October 17, 2009.

Vegan Health. Vitamin B12 Are You Getting it webpage. 2008. Available at: http://www.veganhealth.org/b12/plant. Accessed October 17, 2009.

Cousens G. Vitamin B12 Importance. Living and Raw Foods Website. 1998. Available at: http://www.living-foods.com/articles/b12article.html. Accessed October 17, 2009.

Food coloring and additives
Food and Drug Administration. Microwave Oven Radiation web page. CDRH Consumer Information. 2008. Available at: http://www.fda.gov/RadiationEmittingProducts/ResourcesforYouRadiationEmittingProducts/Consumers/ucm142616.htm. Accessed October 17, 2009.

Meadows M. Plastics and the Microwave. FDA Consumer Magazine website. 2002. Available at: http://fda.gov/fdac/features/2002/602_plastic.html. Accessed October 17, 2009.

Food and Drug Administration. Microwave Ovens. FDA Radiological Health Program website. 2007. Available at: http://www.fda.gov/cdrh/radhealth/products/microwave/html. Accessed October 17, 2009.

Vegan Health. Vitamin B12 Are You Getting it webpage. 2008. Available at: http://www.veganhealth.org/b12/plant. Accessed October 17, 2009.

Cousens G. Vitamin B12 Importance. Living and Raw Foods Website. 1998. Available at: http://www.living-foods.com/articles/b12article.html. Accessed October 17, 2009.

Food Coloring and Additives

Boylstein R, Kanwal R, Piacitelli C. Health Hazard Evaluation Report docket. American Popcorn Company. 2004 Available at: http://www.fda.gov/ohrms/dockets/dockets/06p0379/06p-0379-cp00001-12-NIOSH-vol1.pdf. Accessed October 17, 2009.

United States Department of Agriculture. Food Color Facts. FDA/IFIC Brochure [online]. 1993. Available at: http://www.cfsan.fda.gov/~lrd/colorfac.html. Accessed October 17, 2009.

Glossary

National Institute of Environmental Health Services. Dioxins page. Available at: http://www.niehs.nih.gov/health/topics/agents/dioxins/index.cfm. Accessed October 20, 2009.

Environmental Protection Agency. Polychlorinated Biphenyl page. Available at: http://www.epa.gov/epawaste/hazard/tsd/pcbs/pubs/about.htm. Accessed October 20, 2009

Bruce B DrPH, MPH, RD, FACN, Spiller GA, PhD, DSc, FACN, CNS, Klevay LM MD, Gallagher SA. A Diet High in Whole and Unrefined Foods Favorably Alters Lipids, Antioxidant Defenses, and Colon Function .J Am Coll Nutr. 2000 Feb;19(1):61-7. Available from PubMed. Accessed October 20, 2009.

Bob's Red Mill Natural Foods. Flaxseed Meal page. Available at: http://www.bobsredmill.com/flaxseed-meal.html. Accessed on October 20, 2009.

Bender DA. A Dictionary of Food and Nutrition web page. 2005. Available at: http://www.encyclopedia.com/doc/1O39-phytate.html. Accessed October 20, 2009

Toxi-Free Legacy Coalition. Pollution in People Website. Available at: http://www.pollutioninpeople.org/toxics/pcbs_ddt. Accessed October 20, 2009.

Eskenazi B, Chevrier J, Rosas G. The Pine River Statement: Human Health Consequenses of DDT use. Environmental Health Perspectives. 2009;111(9), 1359-1367.

www.myspace.com/goldigold

Questions about the book?

If you have any questions about the book or recipes please send an email to
customerservice@nattral.com

photo by
Khnum "stic.man" Ibomu

ABOUT THE AUTHOR

As an Author, Certified Holistic Health Counselor, Entrepreneur, Magazine Editor and Crochet Artist, Afya Ibomu has built a dynamic reputation in the past 10 years by consistently delivering on her promise to educate, guide and inspire people to live a healthy, natural, and creative lifestyle.

Growing up in a single-parent home in St. Paul, MN, Afya was born to overcome obstacles and do things her way. She was born with a crooked hip and wore a hip brace for the first 2 years of her life. Afya was very sickly, stricken with allergies, asthma, irritable bowel syndrome (IBS) and a host of other ailments. She was shuttled from doctor to doctor and placed on various medications. When Afya was 15, her mother found an allergy specialist who told her the foods she was eating might be contributing to her health problems. This information and the hip hop song "beef" by KRS-ONE motivated her to stop taking her medications, become a vegetarian, and begin her journey to self-healing.

Afya moved to Brooklyn, NY in the mid 90's, which allowed her to be around some of the most progressive people in the natural health industry. She soon learned about being a vegan, taking herbs, fasting, and live food. Becoming a vegan, led Afya to start cooking again and she began to make her own recipes.

After working in retail for 3 years, Afya quit her head-merchandising job, took a cooking intensive course at the Natural Gourmet Cookery School and started her own catering business called Healthy Soil. She started making gourmet vegan desserts for health food stores around Brooklyn and at international fairs around NYC. Her apple pies became so popular that she was known as the "pie lady".

Yet another twist in Afya's life would bring her to holistic healing. Afya's mother was diagnosed with Multiple Sclerosis. Helping her mother to live a better quality of life through holistic health inspired her to go to the Institute for Integrative Nutrition to become a Certified Holistic Health Counselor. After graduation, She began health counseling, teaching vegan cooking classes, and writing for various magazines, such as; Know Your Health- Minneapolis, MN; Free Magazine –Brooklyn, NY; San Francisco Bayview Newspaper- San Francisco California and Ozone magazine- Atlanta, Ga.

In 2003, Afya was the personal nutritionist for Erykah Badu and her family on the *Worldwide Underground* Tour. That same year, she also produced, directed, and starred in a collaborative TV show for a local cable station in Brooklyn called "Mind, Body and Soulfood".

In 2004, Afya received a publishing deal for her crochet pattern book from The Taunton Press. Her pattern book series, *Get Your Crochet On!; Hip Hats and Cool Caps* and *Fly Tops and Funky Flavas* have sold over 18,000 copies. She and her crochet books have been featured on Good Day Atlanta, AOL Black Voices, in numerous magazines and on HGTV on a show called, Uncommon Threads.

In 2005, she created a nutrition guide called Vegetarian Sources of Protein, currently sold in health food stores around the country.

Afya is currently the CEO of her holistic lifestyle company, Nattral Unlimited, LLC (www. NATTRAL.com), and editor of her monthly online magazine. Nattral.com continues to create new books, crochet designs and products. Afya is also a full time student at Georgia State University studying to become a Registered Dietician. She currently lives in Atlanta, Ga with her husband (stic.man of dead prez) and their son Itwela.

INDEX

A Salad A Day	**pg 98**
Agave Nectar	pg 63
Al dente	pg 163
Al Greens	pg 111
Antibiotics	pg 28
Artificial colors (see food coloring)	pg 70
Aspartame	pg 71
Asthma	pg 33
Basic Pie Crust	**pg 138**
Beans	pg 57-58
Beef	pg 27-30
Beverages	pg 146-149
Go Green Juice	pg 149
Green Goddess Smoothie	pg 148
Green Light Cocktail	pg 149
Hemp My Smoothie	pg 148
Peach Cobbler Smoothie	pg 146
Smoothie Guide	pg 147
Spirulina Shake	pg 146
BHA/BHT	pg 71
Biosolids (sewage sludge)	pg 52
Black strap molasses	pg 63
Boot leg natural sweetener's	pg 64
Braggs liquid amino acids	pg 68
Breads and Desserts	pg 131-145
Basic Pie Crust	pg 138
Carob Brownie Squares	pg 142
Chocolate City Cookies	pg 143
Country Corn Bread	pg 131
East Indian Roti	pg 133
Hood Rich Brownies	pg 141
Hush pups	pg 132
Karamu Corn	pg 145
Nana Muffins	pg 137
NY (no yeast) Pizza Dough	pg 135
Rice Nut Krispies	pg 144
Sweetie Pie	pg 139
The Original "Crown Heights"	
Apple Pie	pg 140
Traditional Pizza Dough	pg 134
Zulu Muffins	pg 136
Breakfast	pg 82-87
Fresh Fruit Kebobs	pg 82
Hearty Breakfast Potatoes	pg 83
Minute Spinach	pg 87
Satisfy My Soul Grits	pg 84
Stacks (pancakes)	pg 85
Sun-day grits	pg 84
Tasty Scrambled Tofu	pg 86
Tempeh Sauxsage	pg 87
Brooklyn Fried Plantains	pg 123
Brown Pride Rice	pg 125
Brown Rice Syrup	pg 63
B-sprouts	pg 114
Buddhist	pg 16
Buffalo Tofu	pg 102
Caffeine	**pg 71,78**
Calcium	pg 42-43
Cancer	pg 27
Cant' Believe This is Squash	pg 119
Carnivore	pg 27
Carob Brownie Squares	pg 142
Casein/asthma	pg 33
Chicken/turkey	pg 31
Chimichanga	pg 104-105
Chlorella	pg 66
Chocolate City Cookies	pg 143
Cinnamon Coconut Cous Cous	pg 126
Classic Corn on the Cob	pg 117
Cloning	pg 30
Coconut Collards	pg 112
Community Coleslaw	pg 95
Complex carbohydrates	pg 53
Condiments	pg 67-68
Braggs liquid amino acids	pg 68
Nutritional yeast	pg 68
Soy Sauce	pg 68
Cooking with Beans	pg 155
Cooking with Tofu	pg 152
Cooking with Whole Grains	pg 154
Cornbread Dressing	pg 129
Country Corn Bread	pg 131
Coup de Grille Veggies	pg 115
Creole Red Beans and Rice	pg 107
Crispy Collard Green Rolls	pg 113
Crispy Fried Cauliflower	pg 110
Cultural grocery stores	pg 50

Curry Lentil Soup	pg 90	
Cutting Tofu	pg 153	
Daal	**pg 108**	
Dairy	pg 16, 32	
DDT	pg 163	
Desserts	pg 138-145	
Basic Pie Crust	pg 138	
Carob Brownie Squares	pg 142	
Chocolate City Cookies	pg 143	
Hood Rich Brownies	pg 141	
Karamu Corn	pg 145	
Rice Nut Krispies	pg 144	
Sweetie Pie	pg 139	
The Original "Crown Heights		
Apple Pie"	pg 140	
Diabetes	pg 62	
Dining Out/ Menu guide	pg 74-79	
Dioxins	pg 163	
Diseases (colon cancer, heart disease,		
high cholesterol, high blood pressure)	pg 27-29	
Down Home Chili	pg 91	
Downer animals	pg 30-31	
East Indian Roti	**pg 133**	
Ecoli and Mad cow	pg 30	
Environment	pg 21, 52	
EPA (Environment Protection Agency)	pg 26	
Essential Fatty Acids (EFA's)	pg 38,60	
Expeller pressed	pg 163	
Expeller pressed oil	pg 60	
Farmer's Market	**pg 48-49**	
Fast Food	pg 78	
Fats and Oils	pg 58-62	
Expeller pressed oil	pg 60	
Fats and Oils	pg 58	
How oils are processed	pg 60	
Hydrogenated/ Partially		
hydrogenated oils	pg 61	
Mono-, poly- and saturated fats,		
EFA's	pg 59-60	
Monounsaturated fat	pg 59	
Oil processing	pg 60	
Polyunsaturated fat	pg 59	
Refined oil	pg 60	
Saturated fat	pg 59	
Trans fats	pg 61	
Unrefined oil	pg 60	
FDA (Food and Drug Administration)	pg 26	
Fermented foods	pg 67	
Filling your basket (shopping)	pg 53	
Fish/seafood	pg 31-32	
Flax seed meal	pg 163	
Flouring a pan	pg 144	
Food Additives	pg 68-71	
Artificial colors (see food coloring)	pg 70	
Aspartame	pg 71	
BHA/BHT	pg 71	
Food Coloring	pg 70	
Gelatin	pg 71	
Hidden Milk and Dairy	pg 70	
High fructose corn syrup	pg 69	
Hydrogenated/ Partially		
hydrogenated oils	pg 70	
Monosodium Glutamate (MSG)	pg 69	
Natural Flavors	pg 71	
Sugar and Sweeteners	pg 71	
Food Coloring	pg 70	
Food Coop	pg 49	
Foods to Limit or Avoid	pg 77-79	
Caffeine	pg 71, 78	
Fast Food	pg 78	
Microwave Foods	pg 78	
Processed foods	pg 77	
Soda and juice drinks	pg 78	
Fresh Fruit Kebobs	pg 82	
Fried Rice	pg 127	
Fruititarian	pg 17	
Fruits/Vegetables	pg 53	
Garvey Salad	**pg 92**	
Gelatin	pg 71	
General References	pg 169-174	
Genetically Modified Food (GMO's)	pg 51	
Glossary	pg 164-165	
Go Green Juice	pg 149	
Gold Grilled Corn	pg 116	
Good Ol' Guac	pg 150	
Grains	pg 125-130	

Brown Pride Rice · pg 125
Cinnamon Coconut Cous Cous · pg 126
Cornbread Dressing · pg 129
Fried Rice · pg 127
Mac-N-Cheez · pg 130
Mo Millet · pg 127
Non whole grains (flour, bread and pasta)
· pg 54
   Wache · pg 128
   Whole grains · pg 53
   (see also Complex Carbohydrates)
Green Goddess Smoothie · pg 148
Green Light Cocktail · pg 149
Grocery Store · pg 49
Growth hormones/antibiotics · pg 28

Halal · **pg 18**
Health advantages · pg 18-21
Health food store · pg 48
Heart disease · pg 28
Hearty Breakfast Potatoes · pg 83
Hemp My Smoothie · pg 149
Herbicide · pg 50
Herbivore · pg 27
Herbs, Spices and Condiments · pg 67-68
Hidden Milk and Dairy · pg 70
High fructose corn syrup · pg 69
Hindu · pg 16
Honey · pg 63
Hood Rich Brownies · pg 141
How oils are processed · pg 60
Hush pups · pg 132
Hydrogenated/ Partially hydrogenated oils · pg 61,70

Iron · **pg 41-2**
Irradiation · pg 52
Ital · pg 18

Kale Salad · **pg 93**
Karamu Corn · pg 145
Kefir · pg 163
Kelp · pg 66
Kombu · pg 66
Kombu, Spirulina, chlorella, nori, seamoss · pg 65-66
Kosher · pg 18

Lactose intolerance · pg 33
Lemongrass Coconut Soup · pg 88
Live/ raw foodist · pg 17

Macrobiotic · **pg 17**
Mac-N-Cheese · pg 130
Main Dishes · pg 99-110
   Buffalo Tofu · pg 102
   Chimichanga · pg 104-105
   Coconut Collards · pg 112
   Creole Red Beans and Rice · pg 107
   Crispy Fried Cauliflowe r · pg 110
   Daal · pg 108
   Pepper Steak · pg 101
   Sauxsage Pizza · pg 109
   Savory Brazilian Sauxsage · pg 100
   Savory Sauxsage Seitan · pg 99
   Southern Fried Tofu · pg 103
   Tofu-Tater Wrap · pg 106
Maple Syrup · pg 63
Mashem' Up · pg 121
Meat and Dairy Question · pg 26-33
Menu Planning · pg 157-158
Microwave pg 78
Minute Spinach · pg 87
Miso · pg 164
Mo Millet · pg 127
Mono-, poly- and saturated fats, EFA's · pg 59-60
Monosodium Glutamate (MSG) · pg 69
Monounsaturated fat · pg 59
Motza Cheez Sauce · pg 150
Mouth Waterin' Butternut Squash · pg 118
Mushroom Gravy · pg 151
My Mama's Potato Salad · pg 97

Nana Muffins · **pg 137**
Natural Flavors · pg 70
Natural Sweetener's (agave nectar, maple syrup, honey, brown rice syrup, black strap molasses, stevia, sucanat)
· pg 62-64
Non whole grains (flour, bread and pasta) · pg 54
Nori · pg 66
Nutrition · pg 36-45
Nutritional yeast · pg 68
Nuts/Seeds · pg 58
NY (no yeast) Pizza Dough · pg 135

Oil processing		**pg 60**
Oils		pg 58-62
Omnivore		pg 27
Organic food		pg 50-53
Oven Roasted Sweet Potato Fries		pg 122
Pasta-fari Salad		**pg 96**
PCB's		pg 50, 164
Peach Cobbler Smoothie		pg 146
Pepper Steak		pg 101
Pesticides/Herbicides		pg 50
Phytates		pg 164
Politics of the Food Industry		pg 26
Polyunsaturated fat		pg 59
Pork		pg 31
Processed foods		pg 54-56, 77, 164
Protein		pg 38-41, 56-58
	Nuts/Seeds	pg 57
	Seitan	pg 58,99
	Soy protein isolate	pg 57
	Sprouted Tofu	pg 57
	Tempeh	pg 57
	Tofu	pg 57
	The Question of Soy	pg 56-57
Pz & Cz		pg 114
Rastafarian		**pg 18**
Reading Labels		pg 68-71
Recipes and More!		pg 81-151
Refined oil		pg 60
Resources		pg 167-174
Restaurants/Traveling		pg 74-77
Rice Nut Krispies		pg 144
Salads		**pg 92-97**
	A Salad A day	pg 98
	Garvey Salad	pg 92
	Kale Salad	pg 93
	My Mama's Potato Salad	pg 97
	Pasta-fari Salad	pg 96
	Sesame Tofu Salad	pg 94
Salmonella		pg 31,52
Satisfy My Soul Grits		pg 84
Saturated fat		pg 59
Sauces and Dips		pg 150-151
	Good Ol' Guac	pg 150

	Motza Cheez Sauce	pg 150
	Mushroom Gravy	pg 151
Sauxsage Pizza		pg 109
Savory Brazilian Sauxsage		pg 100
Savory Sauxsage Seitan		pg 99
Sea vegetable		pg 65-67
	Chlorella	pg 66
	Kelp	pg 66
	See also Kombu	
	Nori	pg 66
	Seamoss	pg 66-67
	Spirulina	pg 66
Seamoss		pg 66-67
Seitan		pg 58,99
Sesame Tofu Salad		pg 94
Shopping List		pg 159-161
Sides		pg 111-130
	Al Greens	pg 111
	B- Sprouts	pg 114
	Brooklyn Fried Plantains	pg 123
	Cant' Believe This is Squash	pg 119
	Cinnamon Coconut Cous Cous	pg 126
	Classic Corn on the Cob	pg 117
	Community Coleslaw	pg 95
	Coup de Grille Veggies	pg 115
	Cornbread Dressing	pg 129
	Crispy Collard Green Rolls	pg 113
	Fried Rice	pg 127
	Gold Grilled Corn	pg 116
	Mac-N-Cheez	pg 130
	Mashem' Up	pg 121
	Mo Millet	pg 127
	Mouth Waterin' Butternut Squash	pg 118
	Oven Roasted Sweet Potato Fries	pg 122
	Pz & Cz	pg 114
	Sweet Baked Beans	pg 124
	Wache	pg 126
	Yams Sweet Yam	pg 120
Soda and juice drinks		pg 78
Soups		pg 88-91
	Curry Lentil Soup	pg 90
	Down Home Chili	pg 91
	Lemongrass Coconut Soup	pg 88
	Vegetable Miso Soup	pg 89
Southern Fried Tofu		pg 103
Soy protein isolate		pg 57

Spirulina Shake	pg 146
Spirulina	pg 66
Stacks (pancakes)	pg 85
Standard American Diet (SAD)	pg 26
Stevia	pg 63
Substitution Basics	pg 162
Sucanat	pg 63
Sugar and Sweeteners	pg 63-64
Sun-day grits	pg 84
Sweet Baked Beans	pg 124
Sweetie Pie	pg 139
Tasty Scrambled Tofu	**pg 86**
Tempeh Sauxsage	pg 87
Tempeh	pg 57
The need for a guide	pg 21-22
The Original "Crown Heights Apple Pie	pg 140
The Question of Soy	pg 56-57
Tofu	pg 57
Tofu-Tater Wrap	pg 106
Tools You Need	pg 156
Traditional Pizza Dough	pg 134
Trans fats	pg 61
Traveling	pg 77
TV	pg 26,79
Types of vegan	pg 16-17
Unrefined oil	**pg 60**
Urban organic farms	pg 49
USDA	pg 26
Vegan	**pg 16**
Vegan FAQ's?	pg 16-23
Vegan Nutrients	pg 35-45
Vegetable Miso Soup	pg 89
Vegetarian	pg 16
Vitamin B12	pg 44, 37
Vitamin D	pg 37,43-44
Wache	**pg 128**
Water, Milks and Beverages	pg 64-65
Whole foods	pg 165
Whole grains	pg 53-54
Yams Sweet Yam	**pg 120**

Zinc	**pg 37,42**
Zulu Muffins	pg 136

www.NATTRAL.com

nattral™

magazine

NAS

Speaks
on Health

The Greatest
Love Of All:
Is loving yourself

Subscribe Today at
www.NATTRAL.com

Issue #5

US $14.95 / $19.95 CAN
ISBN 978-1-60158-941-8

51495

$1

photo by Shannon McCollum

www.NATTRAL.com

Entertainers like Erykah Badu and Common are Getting Their Crochet On!

With over 18,000 copies sold, the *Get Your Crochet On!* pattern book series, provides style and flair for crocheters desperately in search of hip, urban patterns. This two book original collection has patterns for men, women and teens. **Hip Hats and Cool Caps** is the first edition of the series and is a funky collection of 20 caps and crowns that come in a wide range of styles from fedoras to visors to ponytail wraps. **Fly Tops and Funky Flavas**, the second edition, includes tops, bikinis, and tanks, as well as fun accessories like earrings, shoelaces, and belts. For beginner crocheters who love the fashion but don't have the skills, both books include a detailed crochet basics chapter that will have them up and crocheting in no time.

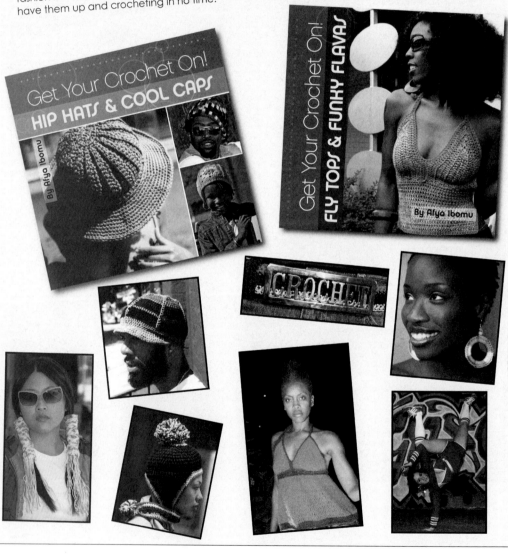

Book Reviews

"I love Afya's hats. They're like crowns and brims of creativity, of genius, of love--they're soulful, something powerful. You'll gotta know that!"
--Common

"Any notion that crochet isn't cool ends right here... Terrific how-to illustrations help first-timers get into the stitching groove while ideas for customizing projects with color, yarn and embellishment are sure to keep you hooked."
- Crochet Today

"Fashion doesn't have to break the bank: Afya Ibomu shows how a skein of yarn and a crochet hook can inexpensively add spice to your wardrobe. These 20 hats for men and women blend together ethnic style and hip-hop chic while keeping construction a breeze!"
- Simply Creative Crochet

"Crochet meets fresh, fabulous headwear in this book...no matter what level you are, we won't blame you keep these cool caps all to yourself."
- Adorn magazine

Get Your Crochet On! Hip Hats and Cool Caps is a must-have book of patterns for every hat or cap you passed on the street and said to yourself, "I want one of those!" This book includes all kinds of cool hats and caps originally designed by the author, who owns a custom-order, Brooklyn-based crochet business and whose creations have appeared in *Jet* and *Complex* magazines. *Get Your Crochet On!* covers the basic crochet stitches, techniques and tools to get you started. This book hopes to capture and express the fresh and innovative styles of a new generation of crochet artists.
--The Daily Advertiser - Lafayette, LA

About Afya

Afya Ibomu is an innovative crochet designer, author, holistic health counselor and entrepreneur. Her crochet creations have adorned such hip hop/rap/soul artists such as Erykah Badu, Common Talib Kweli, Musiq and Dead Prez. She is currently the CEO of her holistic lifestyle company, Nattral Unlimited, LLC (www.NATTRAL.com). She has a monthly online magazine, Nattral Magazine, and is currently working on a vegan cookbook/ guide. She currently attends Georgia State University and is studying to become a Registered Dietician.

Afya can be contacted at:
info@nattral.com
678-637-1815
www.NATTRAL.com
PO Box 310330
Atlanta, Ga 31131

www.NATTRAL.com

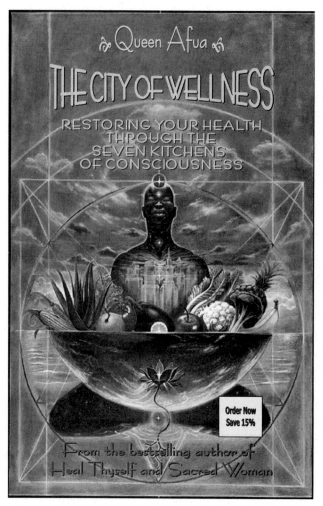

Order Now
Save 15%

The City of Wellness

is an answer to the primal scream from the heart and soul of the African American community. In this groundbreaking volume, holistic health activist, Queen Afua presents a revolutionary "dietary green print " for the malnutrition- obesity-illness epidemic. The City of Wellness, Liberation Diet Plan offers a powerful springboard to wellness because it promotes weight loss, health restoration, and spiritual empowerment.

Praise for the City Of Wellness

Queen Afua has clearly established herself as the "Mother Architect of Healing" The City of Wellness is "Mother's call to come home to our sacred selves. Thank you my sister! I am answering the call"

Iyanla Vanzant

Bestselling Author and Spiritual Coach

For more info:
http://www.myspace.com/queenafua
http://www.queenafuaonline.com/hba/pages/home.htm

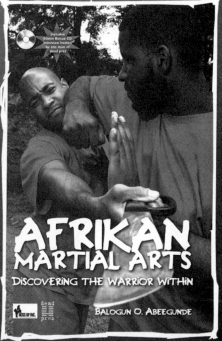